WILHELM HALLER

NEITHER SWORD NOR SCEPTER

The Messianic Way in the Economy and Social Affairs

Texianer Verlag

Neither Sword nor Scepter—The Messianic Way in the
Economy and Social Affairs
by Wilhelm Haller.
ISBN: 978-3-949197-16-1
Original Title in German:
OHNE MACHT UND MANDAT
Der messianische Weg in Wirtschaft und Sozialem
Tuningen: Texianer Verlag 2020
Johannesstrasse 12, D-78609 Tuningen, Germany.
www.texianer.com
Cover image based on: Virgil Solis and monogramist
HWG: Allegorie der Gerechtigkeit; c. 1540/45. (This
work is in the public domain in the United States, and
those countries with a copyright term of life of the
author plus 100 years or less.)

Contents

Foreword....5
Rachel weeps....9
The Unknown Messiah....19
The People of God as Messianic Alternative....39
Living and acting responsibly....65
Freedom and Security....77
The Challenge of the Global Debt Crisis....99
Labor and Income....111
The Right to Issue Directives and Self-Determination....125
The Blindness of The German Protestant Church....143
Capital, Competition and Cooperation....155
Real Estate Ownership and Right of Abode....177
Law and Freedom....185
The Emerging Deity....195

Foreword

At the beginning of the eighties some friends in the Black Forest-Baar region had got together and decided to meet regularly. They were all active in the Christian peace movement. Their common denominator was membership in the German branch of the International Fellowship of Reconciliation. From the very beginning, their encounters were concerned with community building through conversation and a shared evening meal as well as with thematic work that focused mainly on issues of non-violence, the renunciation of power and the topics of the process of conciliation. Eventually the point was reached where the step from talking to taking responsible action beyond the various political actions and activities already engaged in became inevitable. Consequently, the "ecumenical community for social integration *Lebenshaus*[1] e.V." was founded, which set itself the goal of "promoting the idea of community and creating houses in which families can receive people who need help in any way", as it is stated in a *Lebenshaus* leaflet.

In the meantime, this community has long since taken up this work, a work that attempts to have an effect both internally, i.e. concerning the community, and externally, concerning those in need of help in society.

1 Literally, "Life House" – a place for living together. (S.E.)

This is not the place to tell about the history and the workings of the *Lebenshaus*. This must be done elsewhere. Rather, my aim is to report on how in this community—in a way that is unique to me—the theoretical discussion, the attempt at practical implementation, the feedback from both the gratifying and the less gratifying experiences made as well as the resulting theoretical discussion and the subsequent attempt to put the conclusions into practice have led and continue to lead to an incredibly fruitful engagement with social reality and its problems. Here, therefore, people do not live and work at a great distance and with a great demarcation between research-based science, policy-makers who set guidelines and the general public who put them into practice but rather everything is very closely connected and everyone is thus able to become a piece of action research, legislative and executive power—a perpetrator and victim of their own wishes and joint decisions, a laboratory assistant and a test object at the same time.

This process of dealing with the problems of our time did not only take place in the circle of the *Lebenshaus*. Almost parallel to these beginnings, an initiative for the redistribution of work arose, partly with the same people as the sponsors. Later, when the public interest in unemployment and the possibilities of overcoming it diminished more and more, active members began to urge investigation of the deeper causes of the economic problems of our society. This learning process in the *Lebenshaus* was—at least for me and probably for others—supplemented by the discussions in this initiative, especially as far as it concerned and still concerns problems of the economy. Beyond the work in these two groups, it was above all my intensive seminar and lecture work and ensuing discussions that have broadened my insights.

This book is an attempt to put on paper and discuss the harvest that has been gained from this process. It is connected with the invitation to try the same or similar things. As can be easily seen from the individual chapters, they are almost all semantically like protocols of theoretical and practical discussions of particular challenges. Most of them were written in the context of reporting for specific readers or listeners. I arranged and strung them together only afterwards but this did not remove their distinctiveness. The book is therefore less a homogeneous whole than a loose series of essays. Consequently, the individual chapters can also be read on their own and independently of the order in which they are arranged. Thus the book resembles a necklace with stones strung together. The red thread that holds them together is the messianic concern that corresponds to my/our understanding—the service for Rachel, the discipleship of Jesus.

I have long hesitated to add the last chapter to the manuscript, since it has a very strong theological-speculative character. But it occurred to me that all questions about the task and purpose of man and the conclusions that can be drawn from it for our behavior and our systems of order depend very much on our conception of God and our conception of man. Therefore, it seems to me indispensable to raise the question of our image of God and to put my own thoughts on this matter up for discussion. This may put some people off, which is why it might have been better for tactical reasons to omit the chapter, but for the sake of the truth this should probably not be done.

The work connected and documented in this book was made much easier by the fact that a solidarity fund was formed at the beginning of 1991 from the two circles described, which supports my work financially and gives me the freedom to withdraw from organizational consulting, my main source of income, to such an extent that less financially rewarding work can also be accomplished. In this respect the present book is a fruit of this support.

In writing this report, I was burdened by the fact that I have rarely succeeded in doing without terms that refer primarily to men and are therefore the language they use. I must confess that I consider the ways found so far to overcome this plight to be linguistically unsatisfactory. Therefore I must be content to note at this point that of course all terms referring to man, even if they are masculine, mean both genders. I have no doubt that the equality of women and the feminine is indispensable for real justice and for our spiritual progress.

Wilhelm Haller

Rachel weeps

The two female figures Lea and Rachel, wives of Jacob and, like him, of archetypal, i.e. fundamental and often valid significance, were and are so important to me that I repeatedly engage with them.

The story itself is quickly told.

> After Jacob, instigated by his mother, had duped his brother Esau, he became frightened and ran away with the aim of finding security and a wife with Laban, his mother's brother. Even before meeting Laban, he fell in love with Rachel, his younger daughter and, in the course of discussions with his future father-in-law, committed himself to work for her hand in marriage for seven years. At the wedding, however, he had Leah, the older, thrust upon him on the grounds that it was not customary to give away the younger before the older. By necessity, Jacob accepted the arrangement. But because he could not forget Rachel, he committed himself for another seven years to win Rachel as a wife as well. And so, in addition to the unloved Leah, Jacob's beloved Rachel also became his wife.

For an understanding of the archetypal image of the two women, two things are especially important over and above this story.

For one thing, Rachel remained without a child of her own for a long time until she finally gave birth to

Joseph the Dreamer (remember his story in Egypt). The birth of Benjamin, her second child, cost her life. Leah, on the other hand, was a fertile mother with several children of her own.

The second, symbolically of great importance, is the fact that Rachel let her father's household idols go along with her when the family made their hasty exodus. Her trust in her husband's invisible, barely tangible God does not seem to have been so great that she could have done without this physical and tangible reassurance. This tendency towards reassurance seems to be almost symptomatic of the Rachel type—the sensitive, farsighted person who is in search of God and the God-given human community, who in doing so repeatedly succumbs to the temptation of superficial securities.

On the other hand, Lea's picture represents the pragmatic, realistically thinking and acting cosmopolitan, to whom high-flying and far-reaching plans and visions are alien and who is not tormented by any inner insecurity. Leah has many descendants, because the majority feels, thinks and acts in this way. Rachel, on the other hand, becomes the lonely progenitor mother of all messianic dreams and idealistic visions of a better future for humanity and the tasks and aberrations associated with it. She therefore remains childless for a long time. Who would want to get involved with such illusions and dangers in a practical way, if he could avoid it?

The story thus draws two major areas of tension. One represents Rachel's relationship with the invisible God of her husband on the one hand and with the tangible idols of her father on the other hand. The other represents Jacob's relationship with Leah on the one hand and with Rachel on the other. Both areas provide enough tension to make the lives of those who find themselves in them not only agonizing but also fruitful—as long as they become aware of this situation and deal with it. This is what Friedrich Heer means,[2] when he speaks of creative tension people.

The Rachel syndrome is as widespread as the Jacob syndrome. Almost everyone will find painful examples of one or the other, or even both, in their own lives and those of others. Concerning the Rachel syndrome, the following, particularly pictorial example may serve as an example for many others:

Anyone familiar with the history of July 20, 1944 may remember that when Eugen Gerstenmaier[3] was arrested, he carried a New Testament in one pocket of his jacket (symbolic of the God of Jacob) and a pistol in the other (symbolic of Laban's household idol). Nowadays the image of the New Testament—or more correctly: the Greek Bible—and the pistol as Rachel's syndrome is manifested in society as a whole, especially in the military, namely in the German Armed Forces—as far as the people in them feel like Christians. For the individual person, insurance and financial assets have in most cases taken the place of the

2 Austrian philosopher of history (one of his most important books was "Gottes erste Liebe")

3 He was one of the most important heads of the Protestant state church in Württemberg and the Christian Democratic Union (CDU) in the early post-war period (long-standing President of the Bundestag)

Gerstenmaier pistol. Thus according to the image of Rachel, God Mammon has found in us a place of honor.

Thus, the Rachel syndrome becomes not only a danger but a symptom in the sense of the "shadow" described by C. G. Jung[4]. Our experience of God, usually perceived as inadequate, leads in its conflict with the individual state of consciousness that is mainly shaped by the zeitgeist, almost inevitably to the search for other, tangible securities and to poor compromises. The contrast between God and Mammon, of which Jesus speaks, threatens to become a firmly rooted "as well as" in such individuals. No wonder, then, when the churches, just like the churchmen, not only build up enormous reserves but also strive for the greatest financial security imaginable[5]. The decisive factor here is not its ambivalence per se, it is and remains an essential component. The decisive question is how we deal with it? Whether to remain untouched and self-righteous and thus unfruitful or to engage in a painful and fertile confrontation with it that takes us forward.

4 In Jungian psychology, the shadow, (also known as id, shadow aspect, or shadow archetype) is either an unconscious aspect of the personality that the conscious ego does not identify in itself; or the entirety of the unconscious, i.e., everything of which a person is not fully conscious. In short, the shadow is the unknown side. (Wikipedia) Ed.

5 A typical example of this attitude is the public statement made by Dr. Bauer, Finance Officer of the Protestant Regional Church in Württemberg and Senior Church Councilor, during a vicar's conference at the Bad Boll Academy, in which he expressed his concern that the old-age security of church employees beyond 2025 could not be guaranteed today.

These problems bear witness to the unfulfilled dreams and the insatiable longing of such persons. They are usually accompanied by the search for social ideals. It seems that these people, with their desire for security and safety, are particularly susceptible to the temptations of Mammon, so that God seekers easily become gold seekers, gold collectors and gold hoarders. They are thus not only the triggers and bearers of social development but also live in danger of falling prey to various pseudo-safety and pseudo-security, whereby these can of course manifest themselves in other forms than in the addiction to financial security, e.g. in the excessive search for attention from the opposite sex, which seems to apply in particular to men.

Beyond the problem areas outlined above, posterity will probably recognize in today's generation, even the more radical members, the widespread indifference towards the problems of the technically less developed countries and the environment as the Rachel syndrome. The fact that in many respects it is already one second before midnight does not prevent us from displaying a reckless and downright suicidal behavior in our way of doing business, heating our homes, driving our cars, taking out the garbage and many other things. Using biblical terms, this behavior can only be described with the words "hardened hearts", "glued eyes" and "blocked ears" and can be attributed to the Rachel syndrome.

The Jacob syndrome of the relationship with both Leah and Rachel naturally includes the Rachel syndrome. Those who have a closer relationship with Rachel inevitably experience her ambivalence.

In the archetypal meaning of the Jacob syndrome, the fact that Rachel is loved, dreamed of, and courted by the people is particularly important. However, almost everyone comes to terms with the fact that after long years of service, they find themselves betrayed, receiving not the lovable and inspiring yet ambivalent Rachel but the rather average and simple-minded Leah. All too many have had visionary dreams and have even "embarked on the long march through the institutions"[6]. But in the end they become pragmatic and "realistic", adapt to the circumstances and become part of the "establishment" like most others. Thus the old dreams are betrayed and abandoned as unrealistic and the resulting wounding is concealed by superficiality, resignation and cynicism.

The Jacob syndrome became particularly clear in the former GDR (and probably also in other Eastern European states). There, the innovators had often dreamed of liberation for years at great risk and sacrifice and had prepared the ground for and initiated the non-violent revolution that then took place. In the later elections, to their great disappointment, they had to realize that they were overtaken by masses of people on the right and left and that most of their ideas fell victim to the shamelessly exploited greed for the Deutschmark and the consumer mania of our government. The innovators had dreamt of Rachel and worked for her and later had to realize that Leah had taken Rachel's place.

6 A concept of the so-called 68's movement.

In Jeremiah (taken up again by Matthew in connection with the infanticide of Bethlehem) the 31st chapter states:

Thus saith the Lord;
A voice was heard in Ramah,
lamentation, and bitter weeping;
Rahel weeping for her children
refused to be comforted for her children,
because they were not.[7]

Rachel's few children are betrayed, abandoned, sacrificed.

I myself have experienced this situation specifically in my own life story even down to the biblical periods of time and experience it again and again. In the early seventies, I left my former employer together with friends to start a new company with ambitious goals. It was an idealistic, visionary attempt in the sense of the idea of the People of God and thus a service for Rachel. After a few years, however, it became clear that the company was beginning to become a home not for Rachel but for Leah. It took about seven years until this was finally clear and a reorientation and, so to speak, a new commitment was due. It took another seven years until finally the *Lebenshaus* in Trossingen and then my book "Die heilsame Alternative" (The Healing Alternative) prepared a place for Rachel as

7 Wilhelm Haller uses the translation from Martin Buber for all his bible citations in his book. Unfortunately, this wonderful translation is not accessible to the English reader. As a substitute, I have decided to use the King James Bible as my source (except where otherwise stated), despite its inaccuracies, due to its poetical value. (S.E.)

well. But again and again I experience that invitations to lectures or the publication of essays are about "Leah's concerns" and that I have trouble not to neglect or even forget the concerns of "Rachel and her children".

When I was asked by Heyne in the spring of 1989 whether I would write a book about flexible working hours for this publishing house, I initially declined. Although this had been a central topic for me for more than twenty years, I believed that I had finally closed the chapter "Leah" in my life. Eventually it occurred to me that Jacob, too, would remain married not only to Rachel but also to Leah in the long run. And so I agreed and set to work as a service to Leah, the unloved.

This situation reveals a dilemma that many people face, namely a connection, obligation or entanglement involving two different beliefs. As difficult as it may be, the person concerned only fulfills his personal destiny and thus becomes a whole person if he is able to do justice to both emphases in his life, if he serves Leah and Rachel and if he does not overlook the fact that Rachel lets her father's "household idols" accompany her. This, too, must be perceived, taken seriously and accepted.

Normally, however, the situation is usually the opposite than it was with me, since everyone—seemingly inevitably—lives with Leah despite their original Rachel dreams and eventually settles for her, even if at some point in their lives they have pledged loyalty to Rachel. This is not about giving up on Leah. Rather, we should not give up on the painful disappointment of Rachel and not shy away from the additional time of service for her. Only then will we become whole people, pragmatic and visionary at the same time. Unfortunately, this happens all too rarely. Thus Rachel is abandoned and her children are betrayed. "Rachel is waiting", Norbert Lohfink[8] once wrote to me when I introduced him to my life's journey and my relationships with the two wives of Jacob. For whom is she waiting, and with whom is she weeping?

8 A Catholic Old Testament professor in Frankfurt, who became known primarily for his books on the Jewish roots of Christianity.

The Unknown Messiah

In the search for our destiny and the visionary dreams that we were meant to realize, Jesus of Nazareth becomes a signpost—or a stumbling block. However, this is less about the common image of Christ than about the largely unknown Messiah, who is a stranger not only to the Jews but also to most Christians even today. However, there is no direct contrast between the two images. Rather, our image of Christ will have to be supplemented by an image of the Messiah.

The decisive factor here is the fact that Jesus was a Jew and was influenced not only by Jewish traditions but also by his time and environment. Thus the Messianic dream, as he fulfilled it, is peculiar to his people and only his people. Of course other peoples and their religions have also hoped and waited for messianic figures of salvation. The more or less similar expectations of many peoples and cultures have certainly promoted the spread of the Pauline character of the faith in Christ. However, foreign elements, especially from the Greco-Roman cultural area, were undoubtedly adopted.

The adoption of non-Jewish elements, for example, led the Germans, including many of their church leaders, to see in Hitler a Messianic figure to whom they more or less unconditionally submitted, up to the greeting "Heil Hitler". All this took place despite their Christian imprint or perhaps because of it. In any case, this experience makes it clear that their image of the Messiah was unclear and blurred or even completely wrong in decisive points.

What distinguished the Messianic expectation of Judaism in the Jesuanic view is, according to Jewish traditions, already evident in the Hebrew Bible[9] some thousand years before Jesus:

In the decisive story, Samuel is asked by the Jews to provide them with a king, which he does hesitantly and reluctantly. Before that, according to tradition, Samuel had clearly shown the disadvantages of kingship[10]. In the time that followed, this subject did not come to rest. For a thousand years the question of a Messiah, the anointed King of God, as an ideal King who is not an oppressor, remained a fermenting problem. The pregnancy of this "divine thought" in the Jewish people lasted about a thousand years until finally in Jesus the vision became reality.

Israel's stubborn adherence to the ideal of freedom of rule and social justice is all the more astonishing given that all transitions from nomadism to sedentarism and from rural to urban life took place during this period. These are all transitions that usually bring with them a perhaps painful but ultimately uncomplaining adaptation, i.e., submission to a power elite

9 The term "Hebrew Bible" deliberately replaces the usual term "Old Testament" (see also Lohfink, Der nie kündigte Bund, Freiburg, 1989)

10 cf. I Sam. 8

and its privileges. Although this adaptation did not fail to occur in Judaism, the constant preoccupation with the sacred traditions meant that the resulting violation of human dignity never healed. The Jews had quite simply recognized that only the free man, who is not subject to internal or external constraints, can find and fulfill his destiny. They never gave up this knowledge. Erich Fromm writes[11]:

"Precisely because freedom plays such a central role in the value system of the Bible, the liberation from Egypt is the central event in Jewish tradition. It is remarkable that Israel's religious legislation, the commandments issued at Mount Sinai, was preceded by a social revolution, because only free people, not slaves, can receive the Torah".

This was the historical background against which Jesus appeared, the background that undoubtedly influenced and shaped him as well. The story of the Maccabees, who had fulfilled the Messianic expectations of many, was another example of concern to him.

Over one hundred and fifty years earlier, in fact, there had been almost the same historical situation as at the time of Jesus. Whereas with Jesus it was the Romans and their accomplices who suppressed the people, their faith and their worship, before that it was the Greeks. Salvation came at that time through the Maccabees, who, with a successful uprising, liberated the

11 Erich Fromm, Ihr werdet sein wie Gott, Hamburg, 1980. In English: You Shall Be as Gods. A Radical Interpretation of the Old Testament and Its Tradition, New York (Holt, Rinehart and Winston) 1966.

country from the blaspheming Greeks and their collaborators by force of arms and cleansed the temple. Consequently, one of the family of Maccabees was anointed Messianic King and another was anointed Messianic High Priest.

The path of resistance and attempted liberation by force of arms was not only taken by the Maccabees—liberation by force is a contradiction in terms, because it leads to the violent suppression or even death of those who think differently. Until the last great uprising against the Romans by Bar Kochba[12] in 132 A.D., probably more than half a dozen other "Messiahs" tried it in the first two centuries of our era. However, this way had not been very successful, as history testifies. It is also by no means the only one that can be derived from the traditions of the Hebrew Bible. On the contrary. As the prophetic books in particular repeatedly make clear, the hope of the Messiah was actually—or at least also—directed at quite different personalities. However, only a few people saw and wanted to see this, then as now.

Yet there was one—or so we can assume—who questioned things much more critically, who collected the biblical fragments, above all from prophetic sources. These fragments in quiet but forceful language throughout the centuries made it clear again and again that all this was a wrong path to take, even if in the short term it led to success, as with the Maccabees.

12 Bar Kochba was proclaimed Messiah by Rabbi Akiba, who is still highly respected today. He is still considered the last " Prince of Israel" today.

These are all the text passages in which the general tendency to solve social problems by the means of power and violence is contrasted with the lonely path of renunciation of power, non-violence and self-obligation as the only right path.

Thus one of the most important basic concepts for the regulation of human coexistence was and is not only questioned but also replaced by a completely opposite idea—the salutary alternative of the Messiah Jesus. It is still considered undisputed today that the principle of the exercise of power, domination, coercion and violence by a power elite, legitimized as always, is the only way in which a larger number of people can order their living and working together. The overcoming of this theory is of world-historical significance and has enormous consequences for world politics, the extent of which does not seem to have been even remotely grasped to this day.

Only one of the texts supporting the new theory will be quoted here. It is emphasized because, according to the unanimous traditions of the Gospels, it was of such great importance to Jesus that when he entered Jerusalem he staged it so clearly, right down to the last detail, that even the stupidest fellow countryman (then as now) could have understood what Jesus was really about. With Zechariah it says in chapter 9:

> Rejoice greatly, O daughter of Zion;
> shout, O daughter of Jerusalem:
> behold, thy King cometh unto thee:
> he is just, and having salvation;
> lowly, and riding upon an ass,
> and upon a colt the foal of an ass.

And I will cut off the chariot from Ephraim,
and the horse from Jerusalem,
and the battle bow shall be cut off:
and he shall speak peace unto the heathen:
and his dominion shall be from sea even to sea, and from the river even to the ends of the earth.

The King, who is depicted here and is also handed down in the holy scriptures in an unmistakable way, is a completely different King than the Maccabees represented him and the people then and now expected and await him. He is a King of the People and a King of Peace, the promise of God conveyed by the prophet,

"And I will cut off the chariot from Ephraim,
and the horse from Jerusalem,
and the battle bow shall be cut off"[13]

is taken seriously, taking office with unilateral total disarmament and making peace through these " trust building measures". He threatens no one, not even through deterrence, and does not instill fear in anyone. Yes, he does accept the risk of his own terrible downfall in case of failure, as is evident in the further life story of Jesus. So he is a king in the sense of the new theory of renunciation of power and non-violence.

It is incredible and not at all what is taught and conveyed in common Christianity, because only the first

13 Zach. 9,10. Here the translation by Buber in German is particularly important because, in contrast to the Christian standard translation, it makes it clear that this verse represents a divine saying, a divine promise.

part of this text is generally known, as the widely spread Advent song[14] already demonstrates:

Zion's daughter, O rejoice!
Shout aloud, Jerusalem!
Lo, thy King doth come to thee,
Yea, He comes, the Prince of Peace!
Zion's daughter, O rejoice!
Shout aloud, Jerusalem!

Hail, hosanna, David's Son,
Be Thou to Thy people blest!
Thine eternal kingdom come!
Praise be sung to Thee on high!
Hail, hosanna, David's Son,
Be Thou to Thy people blest!

Hail, hosanna, David's Son,
Be Thou welcome, gentle King!
Firmly stands Thy throne of peace,
Thou, the Father's only Son!
Hail, hosanna, David's Son,
Be Thou to Thy people blest!

This is sung up and down the country during the Advent season with eyes transfigured by the glow of candles. Leaning back comfortably in our armchairs, we call upon the King of Peace to found his "eternal kingdom" and generously confirm, "eternally stands your throne of peace", whatever that may mean. But hardly any of those who hear it or even sing it them-

14 Tochter Zion, Freue Dich!, Heinrich Ranke (1798-1876) Translation by H. Brueckner.

selves have the slightest idea of what the text on which the song is based is really about.

As strange and indigestible as the whole thing may seem to us, this is obviously the conviction, the theory that Jesus tried to make clear and to live out in practice. Not very successfully, as we all know, neither then nor now.

How did Jesus deal with the insight that although people welcomed a healer for body, soul, and spirit, they rejected him and his way in political matters and preferred a warlike leader of the Maccabean type, then as now? It must have occurred to him at some time that his contemporaries (as well as ours) celebrated him enthusiastically as a miracle-worker and also received his proclamation of a loving, fatherly God with delight. The political consequences of this, however, remained just as alien to most of his contemporaries as to our own. How did he cope with this, and what consequences did he draw from it?

What must he have asked himself after the first phase of the encounter with the enthusiastic people who, despite all their experience with Jesus, were not ready for the turnaround to renunciation of power and non-violence that was decisive for the history of mankind, thereby abandoning him in one of his most essential concerns? Did he first compare himself with John the Baptist and his proclamation of the punishing God? Looking back, did he remain attached to the fate of the prophet Hananiah, who in a crisis situation of the people, in contrast to Jeremiah, his contemporary and opponent, only proclaimed the merciful and not also the punishing God and had to die for this omission[15]? The comparison was close enough, since the Baptist was more like Jeremiah and Jesus was more like Hananiah. Did he come from Hananiah to Jonah[16], who was sacrificed by the crew of the ship as a shirker from God's mission and had to spend three days in the belly of the fish to mature for his mission to the city of Nineveh?

We do not know in detail but surely Jesus was as fascinated by Jonah as anyone who is concerned about the great repentance, since the story of Jonah remains the only prophetic narrative in the Hebrew (i.e. his) Bible of a great and overwhelming success. Jonah fascinates not only as a stubborn prophet who is not very versatile but also as a very human prophet. He is also a man whose success is probably the result of the unique encounter of an obviously insecure population with a man of God marked by darkness and death, who was capable of causing a great upheaval through his preaching of repentance as a precursor of conversion.

Moreover, as we are told in the Midrash, the returning prophet Elijah said to Jonah's mother: "I will bring the message of salvation and after that your son, the Messiah of Joseph's blood, will appear".[17] According to the oral tradition, which was already alive at the time of Jesus, Jonah was considered a messianic figure,

15 To be read in Jer. 28 ff.
16 The story of Jonah can be read in the book of the same name in the Hebrew Bible.
17 Quoted from Midrash Tehillim based on Weinreb, The Book of Jonah, Zurich, 1970

possibly even one of the two great ones, who as Messiah ben Joseph and Messiah ben David would bring salvation.[18]

According to the two evangelists Matthew and Luke, Jesus repeatedly referred to Jonah and to the great conversion of the people of Nineveh[19]. It is not certain whether the quoted statements actually come from Jesus—Mark at any rate does not report anything about it—but the kinship of both fates is so obvious that it was at least a possibility and a basis for his hope, not only for the evangelists but certainly also for Jesus himself, that his sacrificial journey to Jerusalem would not be useless.

The first phase of Jesus' failed mission was followed by a period of frustration and renewed reflection. It is characterized and shaped by two themes:

On the one hand, by his often suppressed outbursts of rage with the cursing of the Jewish cities[20] in which he had worked, by his inflammatory speeches against the power elites but also by his tears over the doomed city of Jerusalem. In a sense, this first part covers Jesus' emotional reaction to the failed mission.

Here Jesus shows himself as a living human being who allows room for his feelings. For centuries this did not fit the common ideals of either the Christ "without sin" or the "whole" man who does not let his feelings be noticed. Indeed, here Jesus becomes recogniz-

18 See also Zach. 4.

19 Matt. 12, 39 ff, 16,4, Luke 11, 29 ff.

20 His calls to arms (Matt. 11, 21) are obviously nothing more than curses in Aramaic.

able as "the first new man," as Franz Alt rightly describes it.[21]

The other part represents the factual and content-related examination of the future task:

These include the announcements of his death with the invitation to take up the cross. Inwardly connected with this are the statements about the grain of wheat that must die in order to bear fruit. Both points are superimposed and at the same time parts of the now beginning open debate about his "messianity" that simultaneously takes and accepts, even provokes the risk of death from the ruling elite.

Admittedly, it still seems to be disputed in theological research whether Jesus himself had a messianic conception of his own. But even the story of temptation with its argument about the question of power does not make any sense either for a budding itinerant preacher or for a future prophet. It only becomes plausible when we give room to the assumption that Jesus, after his overwhelming experience of God at the baptism in the Jordan River, was virtually swamped by feelings of omnipotence, feelings that for him almost inevitably had to be connected with the idea of being the anointed of God, the Messiah, especially if God is understood above all as the Almighty, as we do to this day. These feelings of omnipotence combined with the everyday experience of the Caesars' omnipotence may have influenced his inner confrontation with his understanding of the messianic tasks in a disturbing manner. However, the described story of temptation

21 Franz Alt, Jesus—der erste neue Mann, Munich 1989

would be meaningless if he wanted to live his life as an itinerant preacher and miracle healer. It would then remain completely without significance.

Also the entry into Jerusalem, obviously staged by Jesus, would be just as senseless as his cleansing of the temple. The same applies to the image of the cross[22], introduced by Jesus at the beginning of the second phase of public relations work. The cross was namely at that time the generally known form of the death penalty of the Roman jurisdiction and was imposed particularly against rebels, thus against political suspects and offenders. The announcement of the risk of the cross had thus for the listeners at that time a completely different meaning than for the average Christian today, who understands this as an invitation to take upon oneself the cross of his life, i.e. also its negative aspects. At that time this statement meant nothing else but this: The one who goes my way, he who takes on the political rulers and must expect to be killed by them for it.

With the announcement of the cross, with the entry into Jerusalem and with the cleansing of the temple—to name only a few but important indications—Jesus takes the probably boldest step of his Messiah mission. Contrary to the already quoted oral tradition, which knew a high priestly Messiah ben Joseph and a royal Messiah ben David, he combined both Messiah images. Whether the death of John the Baptist played a role in this remains an open question. As is well

22 Matt. 10, 38 and 16, 24

known, for many contemporaries and also long after[23] another messianic figure, John the Baptist was almost a rival of Jesus. In any case, it was conceivable during John's lifetime that he could be the high priestly Messiah and Jesus the royal one, a division of tasks that was hardly conceivable after John's death.

It was unthinkable for the world of imagination at that time (as well as for today) that both images would be united in one person. The spectrum of expectations was too wide for that. As Christian history proves, this almost inevitably led to a dualistic split. To this day, in Christianity Jesus is assigned the role of a high priestly Messiah and the fulfillment of the royal role is expected of the Christ who will one day return.

Especially the latter expectation is clearly refuted by Jesus. With his speech about the Kingdom of God that has begun, he takes the ground away from the distant eschatological expectation and shifts our responsibility to the here and now. With the second phase of his public work he underlines this and proves that he was and claimed to be both the high priestly-religious and the royal-political Messiah.

It also shows, however, that renouncing power in critical situations means becoming a victim of power and violence. Tension often rises so high that the step to violence seems inevitable. In such situations, the decision of the politically responsible person is only between being a perpetrator or a victim of violence. Jesus clearly shows and walks the path of the victim and

23 There was still for centuries a Johannine sect in Mesopotamia for whom John the Baptist and not Jesus was the Messiah.

thus unites in a frightening and ingenious way the apparently contradictory and confusing statements of the prophets that led to the two separate concepts of the Messiah. In this way, the suffering Servant of God, in his individual form, becomes essentially the same not only regarding the high priestly-religious Messiah but also the royal-political one.

In addition to this, as a further but rather secondary element, there is the refusal of Jesus to play the "guru" or even the "leader" for enthusiastic followers, that is, for people who are ready to submit unconditionally and personally to a charismatic leader. He had not overcome the temptation in the desert and resisted the enticements of power that came with it, only to succumb to them shortly afterwards. It is therefore not surprising that he repeatedly avoided the crowd, if necessary even fleeing. Moreover, the reference to the risks of succession should help to put a stop to this danger.

All this makes his spiritual path clear—his insecurity and inner distress caused by the new or finally realistically assessed situation, the subsequent phase of inner clarification and the resulting uncompromising attitude. This uncertainty, however, must have gone much deeper than we are usually willing to admit. It becomes clear not only in the story of temptation and the harsh rebuke of Peter when he, after the first great announcement of suffering, obviously suggested alternative paths to him[24]— for example, the life of an inconspicuous itinerant preacher in the country or the

24 Mk. 8 or Matt. 16.

violent resistance as a Messiah in the sense of the Maccabees. It is also recognizable in his not always non-violent statements regarding the question of weapons.

All of this seems to indicate that the Rachel syndrome of "house idols" was for Jesus the question of power and violence, which he was always tempted by but never succumbed to. The last testimony of the biblical traditions for this inner conflict is the story of the "cleansing" of the temple that without doubt, at least for the narrators, is a repetition of the Maccabean temple cleansing in Jesuanic form. The Hanukkah festival is still celebrated in Judaism today to commemorate the Maccabean temple cleansing. Even with us Christians, the memory of this festival has not completely disappeared, since the Jewish custom of the Hanukkah poetry has been adopted by us with the Advent candles, even if most people do not know the roots of this custom.

Presumably, however, Jesus' inner conflict went even further and did not end until the hour before the capture in the Garden of Gethsemane. There Jesus had the last opportunity to decide about his future as a free man. The temptation probably pressed him in two ways. He could have fled to Galilee or—what seemed more compelling in view of the explosive mood in Jerusalem—he could have placed himself at the head of the threatening popular uprising against the Romans and their accomplices. Not because he would have wanted this, but because the "flock without a shepherd" that was also unintentionally provoked by him, was now wandering about without a leader. This totally broke his heart.

His prayer "Not my will, but thy will be done", born of severe inner struggles, refers directly to the quoted word of God from Zechariah[25]. It marks Jesus' inner breakthrough and makes him finally the great Messiah of the renunciation of power and of non-violence, both of which arise from the love for God and for man.

What he had really thought before and what conclusions he drew from it for his further behavior, all this provides a wide field for speculation. How much of it turns out to be a pure projection in the end has to remain open but it is permissible to scrutinize it in order to examine Jesus' motivation for his sacrificial journey to Jerusalem.

An important hint for Jesus' relationship with Jonah is provided by C. G. Jung, who sees in Jonah a prefiguration of Jesus, whereby Jesus unconsciously played a role similar to that of Jonah. But is that all? Is it not conceivable and probable that Jesus himself came to the conclusion that he too must be "sacrificed" and spend "three days in the underworld" in order to achieve great Messianic success through a subsequent new endeavor? Was Jonah perhaps a conscious example and model for his next phase of his life after all? We can only guess and will never know for sure.

25 And I will cut off the chariot from Ephraim, and the horse from Jerusalem, and the battle bow shall be cut off: and he shall speak peace unto the heathen: and his dominion shall be from sea even to sea, and from the river even to the ends of the earth. (Zach. 9.10)

The only question that remains legitimate at the end of the comparison with Jonah is the question of what is legitimate. Was Jesus wrong? Or did the benevolent, fatherly God forsake him because he had quite different, namely punitive plans as in Jeremiah/Hananiah and/or because his people then as now were not ready for the great conversion, which is why the world waits in vain until today for the inspirational model of the people of God according to Isaiah 2 and Micah 4?

Only two options remain. Either Jesus was a Hananiah, who proclaimed a loving God above all else and suppressed the punishing one, with the consequence of a death sentence for him. Then the sacrificial journey to Jerusalem ended objectively-historically and subjectively-psychically with death and destruction for Jesus. Or God is above all a loving God. The option for the Kingdom of God then remains open as a decision of man, because God has long since decided for and not against man—every man. But then Easter and the resurrection will only become reality to the extent that this spirit can rise in us, we overcome our fear and cowardice and our life wants to be an answer to the experienced love of God. This answer is given in the responsible act in the sense of Jesus, that is, in the best Jewish-Messianic tradition. So the decision whether Jesus was a Hananiah or a Jonah is up to us.

If the positive response of mankind is not forthcoming, Easter degenerates into a spring festival, celebrating the awakening, the resurrection of nature, as was and is the custom in all non-Jewish cultures. Quite pretty, but shallow and hopeless—an endless cycle of the ups and downs of the seasons with no salutary way out of captivity.

However, we must not ignore a historical fact. In all probability, Jesus consciously followed the way of Jonah. He deliberately chose, even provoked, the dark time "in the belly of the fish". Was his self sacrifice in vain? Is Nineveh reversed? Do we ourselves repent in sufficiently large numbers? The answer lies within us.

What does this old story mean for us today? A lot or a little? One thing is certain, the beginning of a time of peace, justice and the integrity of creation is in our hands. Disasters are the products of man, even if they are within the limits of their God-given potential. They can only become salutary through an insight arising from contemplation, which then leads to a radical conversion. In this respect, not only the life path of Jonah, but also that of Jesus is seamlessly integrated into the series of pictures of the Exodus from Egypt or the path of the prodigal son, whereby it is ultimately irrelevant to the basic pattern of this journey how much of the path to the low point is self-chosen or self-inflicted or simply fateful without one's own choice or fault. However, it corresponds more to the dignity and greatness of the human being if, as with Jesus and later with Francis of Assisi or Charles de

Foucauld[26], the path is chosen and consciously taken by the individual himself.

Only in our great repentance can the return or coming of the Messiah, expected by many Christians (and Jews), exist. But it probably requires manifold individual experiences of darkness and death to trigger this so urgently needed insight and conversion and to open the door to salvation for mankind. When this happens, then finally the Christian symbol of the cross can change, which until now has correctly represented only the shameful downfall. Then the cross will be transformed by the solar circle around the center of the cross as a sign of the resurrection. Only then will the whole path of man be represented, the path of destruction with the conversion accomplished at the lowest point and the ensuing start of the ascent, the resurrection.

Mysteriously, the ancient Irish had already created the symbol in its entirety. But it disappeared again after the suppression of the Irish Way by the Roman Church[27].

26 Charles Eugène de Foucauld, Viscount of Foucauld, (15 September 1858-1 December 1916), was a cavalry officer in the French Army, then an explorer and geographer, and finally a Catholic priest, hermit who lived among the Tuareg in the Sahara in Algeria. He was assassinated in 1916 and is considered by the Church to be a martyr. His inspiration and writings led to the founding of the Little Brothers of Jesus among other religious congregations. (Wikipedia).

27 The Celtic cross is a form of Christian cross featuring a nimbus or ring that emerged in Ireland, France and Britain in the Early Middle Ages. A type of ringed cross, it became widespread through its use in the stone high crosses erected across the islands, especially in regions evangelized by Irish

This presumably reveals what has been the essential political goal through the centuries, namely the cementing of a sense of sinfulness and a back bent in penitence as a permanent condition. It also promotes the willingness to submit oneself into a subservience that is kept in complete spiritual dependence through a priesthood holding a monopoly on salvation. However, this is probably not much more than speculation. The path that the symbol has taken only suggests that it went downhill from Ireland to Rome, spiritually speaking, with regard to man.

One can assume that for Christianity the time with the holistic symbol of the cross with the sun circle is only just beginning to mature and that for this purpose downfall, conversion and ascent will have to be experienced and accomplished by many.

missionaries, from the 9th through the 12th centuries. (Wikipedia).

The People of God as Messianic Alternative

The 1991 Gulf War once again revealed the divisions among the churches on the issue of military force. On the one hand, the men of the churches (and men in most cases they are) understand that a war can hardly be approved of, not only because of military technology possibilities but also because of the Jesuanic roots of Christianity. They see war as a contradiction to God's will, but they do not know how, in critical situations like the one in the Gulf, to consistently condemn such an ultimately unjust war. Although they complain about the misery caused by it, hardly anyone has the courage to call on the brothers in faith to refuse military service.

The efforts to justify military force are certainly all very pragmatic and politically well justified but it can hardly be denied that they are incompatible with the messianic tasks and goals as interpreted by Jesus. The Messiah of Jesuanic interpretation was and is diametrically opposed to the Roman Caesars and all the efforts legitimized on their path to overcome the problems of human coexistence on a small and large scale through the use of power, domination and coercion, subjugating the dissidents if necessary by force of arms.

We can of course say that Jesus was not only a dreamer but also a nutcase. Therefore, it would be sheer nonsense to follow him in these matters. After all, the renunciation of violence in borderline situations leads to the horrible suppression of the good by the bad, as history has proven time and again. In the past, Jesus himself and also the Jewish people provided a not very encouraging example of this. We should therefore be honest enough to admit that his way of thinking and acting is only partially reasonable and practicable and that in the practical matters of politics, the way of the Caesars seems to us to be more feasible than that of the Messiah. After all, it is more pleasant to beat than to be beaten. With such an attitude of thinking and acting, whether we can still call our faith Christian and base it on Jesus, however, is another question that we are careful not to ask. And so we stick to our hypocrisy, claiming the Jesuanic origin for the Christian faith in spite of all the cover-ups, even though our behavior follows quite clearly the way of the Caesars—albeit perhaps with a heavy heart.

The dichotomy described seems to be all the more blatant the larger the religious community is. This is particularly evident in the attitude of the mainstream churches. The fascination with large numbers seems to force us to make lazy compromises. We are not prepared to forego the support of the broad masses for the sake of a straightforward statement. The willingness to bow to all sides, which is rooted in this, may well please many but we overlook the fact that the biblical message of the Messiah and the People of God is aimed more at the radicalism of a minority than at a more or less indifferent majority. The Messiah is an individual and the People of God a tiny minority in comparison to the whole of humanity. Yet, according to biblical conviction, they should be “a light to enlighten the Gentiles”. Yes, after all, the radical attitude and action of the People of God according to Isaiah 2 and Micah 4 with the famous saying “swords into plowshares” should trigger a pilgrimage of nations and the beginning of peace between the peoples.

The path of incarnation of “divine thoughts” and prophetic visions first and foremost needs individuals and the minority of their communities who are willing to “prepare a place” for these “divine thoughts” so that they can become earthly reality in all their radicality. It seems to be more important to take bigger steps on a small scale than smaller steps on a large scale, or none at all (because we often get stuck in the big speeches and, because of the differences of opinion amongst a large group of people). The path of incarnation needs these pioneering achievements.

It needs the young man who refuses to do military service, even if in the foreseeable future it is unthinkable that in the government in Bonn, for example, the Federal Armed Forces would be abolished or even limited to purely defensive tasks on German soil without nuclear, biological and chemical weapons.

It needs the owners of capital who are willing to lend their money interest-free, even if in the foreseeable future it is unthinkable that an interest-free money economy could emerge in our country or elsewhere.

It needs the founders and operators of third or better one-world stores. Even if in the foreseeable future it is not to be thought of that the large international trade networks would even strive for a fair world economy with appropriate proceeds also for the underprivileged, let alone realize such a thing.

Even if we would see it in purely pragmatic terms that the greater step in the small would not bring more than the small step in the great, the first conforms to the biblical, the Messianic way of the People of God, and not the second does not. We can confidently leave the second one to the pragmatists of power and the politicians. If—to quote Erhard Eppler—with the more radical "pioneers" it could be said, "Here I stand, I can do no other", with the politicians it would probably be, "Here I stand, I can do the other". That is, they declare themselves capable of change. If the new, which wants to grow and take on earthly form, were to take hold of more and more people in a kind of chain reaction, then politicians would eventually make the new way of thinking their policy too. So it is less a matter of making common cause with politicians than of preceding them and creating the conditions for the realization of desirable examples, even if the prospects for this are often enough not very rosy.

By the way, it has to be pointed out that it is not so much a question of an "either—or" as of a "both—and". The work in the great and by the great is thus not to be denigrated here in principle. Rather it must become clear that the first-mentioned way that up to now has been grossly neglected or not seen at all and consequently seldom taken, is the actual Messianic way.

What this path could look like can be easily explained using a simple example:

Let us assume that you would come to the conclusion that a new property law with neutralized land ownership is an essential prerequisite for more justice in the housing question. There are basically two ways to turn this insight into reality:

You can turn to the big party that is close to your political convictions and try to get your ideas included in the basic catalog of that party. As we all know from experience, this is a process that can take many years. If you now have the misfortune of sympathizing with a party that is in opposition, even if your efforts over the years are successful, it will mean that the statement of principles with your ideas will remain in a dark opposition drawer for years to come. Even if your party should come to power, it cannot be ruled out, and is even likely, that it will do so in coalition with another party that may reject your ideas, which is why they will not be included in the coalition agreements and therefore remain in a drawer for further years without anything happening in your favor. In the worst case, it may take many decades before the insights of minorities, however good and right, become political reality.

The salutary alternative of the Messianic way does not exclude the described attempt, as long as it is limited to a serving and advisory function and does not attempt to exercise power and pressure. But its main concern would be that you simply set up a foundation or a non-profit association together with like-minded people (the smallest cell of the "People of God") in the spirit of your concern (no one will seriously prevent you from doing so) and in public conversation advocate that people transfer their property rights to your foundation by their own volition as an act of personal conversion (and that is what it is all about).[28] According to the promise of Isaiah 2 and Micah 4, you can hope that the fascination of these examples will spread and cause more and more people to take similar steps long before corresponding laws are passed in government as coercive measures for everyone. They would thus prepare a site as a basis for the miracle of repentance to happen.

Whoever sees themselves as a member of the messianic people of God is above all committed to the future of God on this earth. In the spirit of Jesus' request in the Lord's Prayer, "Thy will be done on earth as it is in heaven," it is necessary to create places in the earthly realm for the Spirit of God, who is urging for peace and justice, and to create places in which His intentions can become more and more reality. This is the service for Rachel, which gives meaning, purpose, fulfillment and dignity to the human being. But at the price of segregation and also of inner homelessness, which is already very clear in Jesus, who not only said of himself that he "had not where to lay his head" but also that "his kingdom was not of this world". With this he did not mean, or at any rate did not only refer to the "heavenly hosts and realms" but just the future, the future here on earth, which is rooted in the transcendent. In a similar way this is probably meant in

28 See also the chapter on property ownership later in this book.

Paul's words: "We have no lasting city here, but we seek the future one"[29].

Jesus and also Paul are—according to Friedrich Weinreb—true Hebrews. Weinreb writes[30]:

"... this is what (the Hebrew word—author's note) EBER means "from the other side", that is, from another world. The Hebrew, the "Iwri"—as it they are actually called—has thus, seen from this world, come from another world. One who is a stranger in this world—wherever he goes he takes... restlessness with him. He stands in contrast to the "normal" course of things, he crushes the gods. He seems to set up a sign for this world that there is something else. He is awakening this world for the other world."

"From another world, for another world," that is the motto of their life, even if the other is not much more than a promise, a promise, a hope.

The "Hebrews" are thus the bearers of the change of this worldly reality born of the Spirit of God. They are the children of Rachel. But they are not only as members of a certain race or religion. They are so because they are rooted in another reality, regardless of their origin or their affiliation, and because they are obliged to divine utopias and prophetic visions for this world out of their longing for God, for the Infinite, for the divine utopias pressing for incarnation, for earthly reality.

But that is not all. For it is not only about the individual human being and his destiny. It is not only about

29 Hebr. 13,14

30 Friedrich Weinreb, Die Rolle Esther, Bern, 1980.

man as an individual person, but also about the human community.

In Jesus, perhaps for the first time clearly observable, is man's departure from collectivity into individuality (Hanna Wolff calls him in this sense the "anti-collective Jesus"[31]). As is evident everywhere, this leads to an overemphasis on the individual, to his individual greatness and dignity but also to his isolation, his helplessness and his forlornness. The "we" is, however, indispensable for the "I". Hanna Wolf also sees this and writes: Jesus' "But I say to you" leads out of this undifferentiated inability to relate and thus makes true community possible in the first place... Out of the becoming of the I now arises a We of a higher order. Instead of the pre-personal "we" piety, a real, consciously differentiated "we-community" becomes possible in the first place.

This community building as a compelling religious and political necessity was also a concern of Jesus. Building on the traditions of his people, he gave an answer to the question, which always the first to arise, of the enforcement and enforceability of political will upon his way of renouncing power and violence:

Those who refrain from using the instruments of power, domination and violence to enforce their political will have as their political "disposable assets" not the target groups of the population, who are more or

31 This is a misleading description by Hanna Wolff, since Jesus criticizes traditional family structures but explicitly promotes new forms of community building. (Hanna Wolff, Neuer Wein—Alte Schläuche, Stuttgart, 1981).

less seduced by electoral tactics, but instead only themselves, realistically speaking. What remains for them to do if they still want to achieve their political goals? First, they will seek out like-minded people and second, they will try to convince others on the level of equal rights and equal rank in the discussion. They will not exert pressure or coercion. It was in this sense that Jesus sent out his disciples. In Matthew, the tenth chapter can be read:

"And into whatsoever city or town ye shall enter, enquire who in it is worthy... And whosoever shall not receive you, nor hear your words, when ye depart out of that house or city, shake off the dust of your feet."

In this way, like-minded people are both sought and collected. Together they form the working group for the realization of the common political goals. They are sower and seedbed at the same time. According to Jesuanic politics, they do not appear as a party that—if necessary in coalition with others who have similar political goals—tries to come to power in order to assert its political convictions even against the will of the rest, large or small. Rather, they see themselves together as a pioneering society whose task it is to realize their political will within their own structures while renouncing power and mandate, i.e. to make themselves individually and collectively responsible for conversion and change. In this way, they resemble the pioneer plants that are the first to colonize the soil after natural disasters or in inhospitable areas, thus preparing it for colonization by others.

The primary goal of political work in the sense of Jesus is thus not the nation-state macro-society, but the formation of an alternative society within the macro-society, unrestricted by its borders. The first step is the formation of base communities, i.e. communities of manageable solidarity. But since many social problems are too big to be solved within individual communities —let us only think of the North-South conflict—a conscious second step is needed—the global networking of these communities. Using our current terminology, we would say that we are talking about the network of a transnational alternative society.

The change of the rather rejecting and hostile macro-society is only a secondary, indirect goal, as the Zechariah text makes clear. The decisive contribution to world peace that is spoken of there is the unilateral disarmament within Israel's "alternative pioneer society". The idea of changing the political landscape of the major societies is not based on the means of power. The change should therefore not be forced. It is no more than an offer based on a concrete social example. This offer leaves the person being addressed the freedom of choice to decide for or against it, however painful the result of such a decision may be for all concerned. The liberty addressed here is a central concern of the Bible, as it is stated already in the preamble to the Ten Commandments or better said, the ten liberties[32]: "I am your God, who frees you".

Belonging to this transnational alternative pioneering society requires an independent identity, a civic consciousness independent of citizenship and a corre-

32 A term that Ernst Lange introduced with his book "Die zehn Freiheiten" —The Ten Freedoms.

sponding ethic. Both are almost completely lacking today. For Jesus the matter was simple. According to Isaiah 2, God's command to transform Zion, the city on the mountain, into the world, triggered by the concrete example of the people of God. In concrete terms, this means that the "directive of God", which is laid down in the Mosaic laws—the Mosaic legal order—must be realized in an exemplary manner in the Messianic pioneer society before the pilgrimage of nations described there before the goal of its completion can be expected. This Mosaic legal system is partly unattained to this day. For example, the law concerning foreigners could of course only be realized by the Jews themselves, because it was only the Jews who made the effort. For this reason, Jesus quite deliberately addressed himself only to the Jews and consistently refused to address non-Jews as well. This is demonstrated by the story of the encounter with the Canaanite woman. According to Matthew 15:24, he at first mercilessly rejected her with the words, "I have been sent only to the lost flock, the people of Israel."Even when he sent his disciples to do independent political-religious work, he strictly instructed them according to Matthew 10, "Avoid the places where gentiles live, do not go to the cities of Samaria either, but go to the lost flock, the house of Israel."

As far as Jesus was concerned, the Gentiles were unsuitable for the Messianic pioneer society. This was not because they were inferior but simply because they pursued other goals than the fulfillment of the legal order of God according to the Mosaic laws in their society, the basis for the Kingdom of God. After all, the non-Jews did not even know them. The central concern of Judaism, as servants and instruments of God, to create the preconditions for the Kingdom of God on earth[33] with peace and justice, was completely foreign to them, at least in its essential fundamentals. It is still the case today, as the main streams of Christianity prove.

Jesus' conviction was initially also adopted by the first Messianic congregations within Judaism. However, these were then plunged into considerable moral conflict as more and more non-Jews joined the movement. James, the biological brother of Jesus, thus also of Davidic descent, had taken over the leadership of the Messianic movement within Judaism as "Prince Regent" until the expected return of Jesus. He finally passed the verdict that non-Jews could be admitted, provided that they submitted to the so-called Noachite laws[34] and thus fulfilled the minimum requirements for the realization of a social legal order according to God's instructions[35].

33 In Christianity misunderstandably usually referred to as the kingdom of heaven.

34 Refer to chapter 15 of the Acts of the Apostles.

35 These are the laws which according to tradition date from the time of God's first covenant with man after the Flood. They apply to all people, including non-Jews, and are set in the time before Moses and before the history of Sinai (see also Genesis, 9). They are handed down in Judaism in various numbers and to varying degrees, so that it is not certain whether the evangelist was not aware of all of them, or whether the scope described was in fact the generally valid one at the time.

Paul did not go far enough with this decision of the central council in Jerusalem. This was due to his mystical over-zealousness and his origin and influence by Greek culture. In his famous Epistle to the Romans, he declared the law as such to be superfluous. In the third chapter, he writes, "God has acted in a way that corresponds to his nature. He has himself ensured that men can stand before him. He has set the law aside and wants to accept people if they trust solely and **completely** in what he has done through Jesus Christ…"[36]

Unfortunately, Paul completely overlooked the fact that the law of which he speaks not only contained all sorts of ritual orders and perhaps really superfluous

36 This footnote can be found in a sermon Reformationstag October 31, 1999 by Bishop Dr. Sigisbert Kraft: https://www.ekidi.de/xx_predigt/1025_120_000.html.
I have chosen here to translate based on this text which differs somewhat from the KJV in order to maintain the point being made: "But now the righteousness of God apart from the law is manifested, being witnessed by the Law and the Prophets, even the righteousness of God, which is by faith of Jesus Christ, unto all and upon all those who believe. For there is no difference, for all have sinned and come short of the glory of God, being justified freely by His grace through the redemption that is in Christ Jesus. Him God hath set forth to be a propitiation through faith in His blood, to declare His righteousness for the remission of sins that are past, through the forbearance of God; to declare, I say, at this time, His righteousness: that He might be just, and the justifier of him that believeth in Jesus. Where is boasting then? It is excluded. By what law? Of works? Nay, but by the law of faith. Therefore we conclude that a man is justified by faith apart from the deeds of the law." (S.E.)

constraints and unfulfillable duties, but also the greatest social legal order that the Mediterranean culture has produced. Paul threw the baby out with the bath water. After his unintentional legitimation of unbridled restraint and social chaos, which his listeners and readers perceived as such, he had no choice but to drive his confused flock into the fold of the Roman legal order. In many respects this legal order was and is diametrically opposed to the Jewish one. It is therefore not surprising that his statement in the 13th chapter of the same letter to the Romans still causes great confusion in Christianity today. There he writes, in logical consistency to his preceding conviction quoted above, "Everyone should submit to the authority of the state. For there is no state power that is not conferred by God. Whoever rebels against the authority of the state resists the order of God and will be punished for it."

The abolition of the Jewish law, i.e. the Jewish legal order with its ideal of freedom of rule and solidarity with the "widows and orphans", i.e. the weak members of society, left Paul with only the recommendation of submission to the Roman legal system. This recommendation emphasized the central state omnipotence and made private property absolute. Thus the seeds were already sown for the abandonment of the idea of a people of God as an autonomous pioneering society with an independent legal system shaped by the Jewish Messianic tradition.

In contrast, the Jewish communities, or those influenced by Jerusalem, saw themselves as a social and political movement within Judaism. They regarded themselves as something like a semi-autonomous pioneer society with a legal system based on the Mosaic laws. In this system, the teachings of Jesus as the continuation and final form of this legal order were to a certain extent developed into the Basic Law and the constitution of the people of God. This becomes clear, for example, in the structure of the Gospel of Matthew, which is characterized by the Jewish spirit—even though the author himself was in all probability not a Jew with a Hebrew mother tongue[37]. In this book, Jesus is presented as the new Moses. The main propositions of Jesus, which are summarized in the Sermon on the Mount, form an analogy to the Mosaic legislation at Sinai, or better still, as its continuation and final form.

The close relationship to Moses and his followers is already apparent in the name. The Hebrew basic form of the name is the same for Jesus and for Joshua, the historical successor of Moses, namely Jehoshua. Thus the relationship to Moses and to the task of continuing the mission of Moses is established from the very beginning with the name.

This is clearly about a social legal order for God's people and God's kingdom in the Messianic age, that is, for the time of the beginning of God's reign.

37 This can be recognized by the fact that he succumbs to translation errors (Young Woman—Virgin, Is. 7.14–Matt. 1.23) as well as being unfamiliar with the peculiarities of the Hebrew language, which is why Jesus, according to his report, enters Jerusalem with two donkeys (Matt. 21.2), while the reference text (Zech. 9.9) only repeats the speech about an ass in a typically Hebrew parallelism, thus emphasizing the statement.

The Pauline diversion[38], on the other hand, which of course was not deliberately intended by Paul the Jew, led to the Messianic movement. This movement was originally characterized by a Jewish, domination-free sense of justice that was subsequently overwhelmed by Roman imperialist ideas of justice. The general political assimilation and subjugation was formally sealed with the Constantinian turning point in the 4th century. The suppression of Jewish legal principles only came to an end in the 6th century under Emperor Justinian, with the introduction of the CORPUS IURIS CIVILIS that was built on pre-Christian Roman legal principles. Consequently, the prohibition of the publication and distribution of the Talmud was connected with this. In this way, the Jewish sense of justice in the Christian Occident was finally denied access to the Talmud. This is how it has remained until the present day. The imperialist Roman Caesar had thus crucified the Jewish Messiah for the second time. The second resurrection, however, has not yet taken place, at least not within the major churches.

Nevertheless, it cannot be overlooked that the spirit that shaped Jesus continued to work within Judaism. The destruction of the temple led not only to the abolition of the temple and sacrificial cult, whose roots can already be observed in the prophets. It also led—politically highly significant—to the abolition of the central omnipotence of the Jerusalem priesthood with

38 This change of course must be ascribed to Paul, even though it may have already been observed with the first assimilated non-Hebrew Jewish Christians in Antioch.

its monopoly on salvation. Consequently it led to the decentralization of the spiritual authority with synagogues and quasi Jewish colleges, which were formed in various places with wise men and scholars at their centers. It also led to an increased formation of the rabbinate.

As is well known, rabbis did not only take on the role of spiritual leaders in the parishes, as in Christian parishes pastors and priests do. They were and to some extent still are judges and arbitrators in disputes of a non-religious nature. This was a continuation of the tradition that had faded into the background in history with the realization of kingship by Samuel, the last great "judge". For many, such as the Jewish-American writer Isaak B. Singer[39], this system of law and order is still regarded today as an ideal to be realized anew in a reformed form, i.e. without a relapse into ultra-orthodox spiritual rule.

Indeed, for many centuries Judaism had uniquely preserved its national-religious existence without national territorial integrity, which would have required a military power apparatus, and without a central religious authority, such as the Pope and the Vatican still represent for the Catholic Church today. Here, then, a large piece of "divine utopia" has become reality, a utopia whose significance for all of humanity only seems to become fully clear in our time.

39 Isaac Bashevis Singer; November 21, 1902–July 24, 1991) was a Polish-American writer in Yiddish, awarded the Nobel Prize in Literature in 1978. (Wikipedia)

Jesuanic politics, as it found its expression in the Sermon on the Mount and how it intends to become a reality within the pioneering society of a people of God, renouncing power, dominion and violence, fell into oblivion. It was only taken up by marginalized social groups, which is why these groups were frequently brutally persecuted—also and especially by the main stream churches as a stumbling block to the Sermon on the Mount.

This brings us back to the starting point. Jesuanic politics. which renounces the exercise of power and domination. It can only be carried out by the community of like-minded people and the hope that this community will grow, that it will connect with others in a network and that it will finally become an exemplary model for the nation-state societies.

This path to achieving political goals thus begins with self-experiment and self-obligation, both individually and collectively. The collective dimension cannot be valued highly enough. After all, it is primarily about social problems and thus about the solidarity-based community and society, which at some point must take on global dimensions. These are collective tasks that presuppose, however, an independent, autonomous identity. For lack of corresponding images, this identity can only be compared to a "national" one, even if it is transnational.

An essay entitled "Der Mensch im Kursverfall" ("Man in Decline"), published by Wolfgang Huber in PUBLIK FORUM in the fall of 1988, shows just how much our ideas on this issue remain blurred. After a gloomy but admirably realistic stocktaking, he concludes with the sentence:

"If we can summon up the strength for such responsible self-limitation, then there could really be a turn towards the future, which would be a real alternative to the neoconservative thinking of the present."

Who does Huber mean by "we", who is addressed? Does he mean us as citizens of the large national societies of the industrialized countries? If so, then he and we as his readers should have the courage to admit to ourselves that his closing remarks are nothing more than a rhetorical appeal, which any realistic observer of the development knows will not go unheard but will have no consequences. Political reformism, which had set itself the solidarity demanded by Huber as its goal, is as good as dead. The political goals in Western Europe for the foreseeable future are to consolidate and strengthen their own positions for the economic struggles in the coming European internal market. This means accelerating technical progress, promoting economic growth and the accumulation of monetary and capital assets—all this at almost any price and certainly at the price of further weakening the social safety net. One must only listen to the demands of employers and the promises made to them by our ministers of economic affairs.

So who is the addressee of Huber's appeal?

We should finally have the courage to abandon political naivety with its hope for the rapid reform of the big national societies as a direct result of the political pleas and urges of a responsible minority and to find back to the biblical realism according to which, for the time being, only "a remnant repents". The "real alternative" of which Huber speaks can be realized for the time being only in the alternative society of the "People of God". But according to the biblical promise, salvation is to proceed from this very place. So let us build on this.

For this purpose, however, it is necessary that those touched by the call really recognize themselves as those called out. They also need to become aware that this alternative society must emerge as an independent, autonomous society with its own identity if it is to grow into a pioneering society with the tasks described. This is already clearly visible in the economy as an example. As long as alternative companies are expected to be able to assert themselves in the competition of the international economy according to its rules, most of them will face an unsolvable task. Only when we have achieved a relationship of solidarity between consumers and producers, where mutual consideration for the vital interests of the other party becomes the yardstick, will we be on the right track. However, this may mean accepting higher prices and other inconveniences. It is simply a joke to claim that shopping with friends in the alternative must not only be better and more sensible but also cheaper. Usually the opposite is the case. For many people, their selfish market economy thinking with its objective of achieving the highest possible prices for their own work and paying the lowest possible prices for external work becomes an insurmountable hurdle and a pitfall.

We must learn to distinguish, in the sense of an autonomous pioneer society, between a kind of "domestic economy" within this pioneer society and "foreign trade" with other economic units. It is important to understand that in an initially very weak "domestic economy", the value added must come primarily from "foreign trade". This applies both to wage labor and to the independent management of goods and services. Consequently, the number of those who can be supplied "domestically" in economic dependence will remain small at first. Yet it can grow to the extent that we understand that while many must earn their income in "foreign trade", as much as possible should be spent in "domestic trade".

This can be best understood using the example of the non-assimilated Jews in exile in past centuries. Not only did they provide each other with all kinds of social security and support, they also helped and supported each other in economic life. Foreign trade with the non-Jews, on the other hand, was primarily a source of income and earnings for them, also for the economic strengthening of the community. Of course, there were excesses in this way of thinking and acting. However, self-interest should not be permitted to degenerate into an end in itself. As long as the goal of making the People of God a pioneering society and economically viable, combined with fairness and openness towards the general public, with regard to concerns and goals as well as the concrete figures of "economic and social policy", then this path is good and right.

Such calls remain helpless, even paralyzing, if, however, as this is to be understood from Wolfgang Huber's report (perhaps he meant it differently), Christianity and national societies are almost congruent with —politically speaking—at best blurred boundaries. For who, for heaven's sake, is to have the strength to achieve the turnaround described in the ponderous colossus of the national large-scale society. All the more so since politics and economics in this large-scale society obey the thinking and laws of the Caesars rather than those of the Messiah?

Let us take the example of Norbert Blüm[40], who in his time as head of the Christian social committees was jointly responsible for the development and elaboration of laudable social projects. He was not only open to all kinds of social renewal but also became its eloquent representative. What has become of him?

Who among us could claim that he would not have the same fate in a similar situation? I am afraid that the new, the aspirational ones " at the top" cannot attain governmental legal force if they have not previously

40 Norbert Blüm (21 July 1935–23 April 2020) was a German politician who served as a federal legislator from North Rhine-Westphalia, chairman of the CDU North Rhine-Westphalia (1987–1999), and Minister of Labour and Social Affairs. Blüm adhered to Christian values and belonged to the left wing of the generally centre-right CDU. Blüm was strongly influenced by the Jesuit social philosopher Oswald von Nell-Breuning, one of the founders of the modern Catholic social teaching who lectured in Frankfurt. Nell-Breuning taught Blüm about the main three pillars "subsidiarity", "solidarity" and "charity". After his departure from the Bundestag in 2002, he continued to comment on political issues publicly. Because of his criticism of Israel in the Middle East conflict, he was sometimes accused of antisemitism, which he rejected. (from wikipedia).

become a sufficiently tangible reality "at the bottom". The experiences of the recent past prove it again and again.

I only have to think of how only a few years ago the efforts of open-minded minorities to protect the environment and to live and act in an environmentally sound manner were insulted and ridiculed by the power elites at all levels. Today, these same elites advocate this as part of their policies, proving once again that this insight is correct.

What applies to the question of environmental protection is equally applicable to the economy and all other questions of social coexistence. However, the challenges are so complex and difficult that in many cases the reality of a pioneering society as a transnational network of largely autonomous communities and municipalities is indispensable. Individuals can no longer lay the basis of change solely through their responsible actions. It is not only the Bible that provides the necessary guidelines for this. We can also learn a lot outside of the Bible. For example, in non-white, technically underdeveloped cultures where the process of individualization has not destroyed all thinking and acting in communal structures as in the Western world. It is not a matter of abandoning the one in favor of the other. Rather, it is a matter of combining the two in the best possible way and trying to make room for the individual's urge for freedom as well as his longing for security in the community. Thus it is not about abandoning the one in favor of the other but rather about trying to create an economic system that makes "competition and cooperation" possible in equal measure.

The concept of a Messiah in the Jesuanic interpretation and of a people of God corresponding to this interpretation seems particularly plausible in the light of the hypothesis of the causes of formation developed by the English biologist Rupert Sheldrake. In this theory, "morphic" or "morphogenetic fields" of all forms from crystal to human behavior play a decisive role. As the title of his latest book suggests[41], they represent a kind of memory of nature. Sheldrake writes: "This collective memory is of a cumulative character, i.e. it becomes more and more pronounced through repetition, so that we can say that the nature or peculiarity of things is the result of a habitualization process, i.e. habit. Since memory is not only collective but also cumulative, the more individuals are familiar with it, the easier it is to learn completely new skills".

Conversely, this means—and this is the decisive point of Sheldrake's theory for our concern—that learning and practicing a completely new behavioral pattern. This represents an extraordinarily painful and laborious new beginning for humans, because a "morphic field" must first be created for it—albeit from "a latent possibility" (Sheldrake). This is nothing other than the process of incarnation described in the Bible, which the translation by Martin Luther at the beginning of John's Gospel makes particularly clear, "The Word be-

41 Rupert Sheldrake, Das Gedächtnis der Natur, München, 1989. (Presence of the Past, Icon Books, 2011).

came flesh and dwelt among us".[42] This incarnation process encompasses not only the incarnation of God in Jesus, but the entire process of creation, progressing from the physical to the psychological. It also encompasses human behavior and wants to change it not with power, coercion and violence but through an inherent human longing for the fulfillment of "latent possibilities". This yearning becomes the decisive driving force. In this process, the independent contribution of the human being becomes indispensable as an answer to this aspiration.

According to Sheldrake, the repetitions of past pioneering work become progressively easier as their morphic field becomes stronger and stronger.

In order to make the theory even more understandable despite its brevity, Rupert Sheldrake is quoted again from the book mentioned above:

"Morphic fields, like the known fields of physics, are non-material force zones that propagate in space and persist in time.... They are potential organizational patterns.... The process by which the past becomes the present within a morphic field is called morphic resonance."

Of course, it is not possible to describe the content of this complex theory in detail or even to present the wealth of evidence for it and the respective reservations here. The only thing that seems important in our context is the fact that obviously the creative pioneering work and its repetition is of extraordinary importance. In fact, it is the decisive key role. Without

42 John 1.14.

power, coercion and violence, it creates new forms and new norms, which make further repetition up to the general self-evidence increasingly easier. Thus, finally, the great prophetic visions, such as those according to Isaiah 2 and Micah 4, can become reality. This means that the earthly reality is able to come closer and closer to the "divine utopias", i.e. the latent possibilities.

US studies on the process of implementing social innovations point in the same direction. They say that 5% of the population is enough to firmly root an idea ("embedded" is the American term). Once the idea has reached 20% of the population, it becomes unstoppable. However, it is not clear how long these two steps will take. In any case, we do not need a majority from the outset, which we stare at with our power-political conditioning like a rabbit at a snake. Anything else seems to most of us not to be worth the trouble.

Perhaps we finally understand how modern, forward-looking, indispensable and above all salutary the concept of God's people as a pioneering society for all mankind really is.

Living and acting responsibly

In contrast to the official program, the annual conference of the German branch of the International Fellowship of Reconciliation in 1986 was marked by the Chernobyl catastrophe, which occurred only a few days earlier. In addition to emerging desperation and helplessness, there was a great need to shake up those in positions of responsibility in politics and business. They were about to go over to the usual agenda in a cloak of silence and trivialization with a shrug of the shoulders. It was this necessary to shake them up and make them take serious consequences from the catastrophe by sending parcels of rotten vegetables to the politicians and nuclear power plant operators. The more militant ones fended off the temptation to resist with more brutal means and even to knock down a power pylon.

Years later, we must ask ourselves: What has remained—with us and with those responsible?

If we take a serious look at the situation then and now and all the actions and activities associated with it, it is noticeable that a holistic concept of changing society with ourselves as the primary targets of change was largely lacking and is still lacking today.

It seems to me that we will always run out of the stamina and endurance we need in order to change society, if we aim above all to change the outside world.

We are more likely to gain the necessary stamina if our idea of the necessary change is comprehensive. To be so, it must correspond to the Messianicity" of Jesus, which had both an inner, religious-spiritual aspect—namely the high priestly one—and an external, political aspect—namely the royal one. As this was already clear with Jesus, it is always about an internal and an external aspect. Ideally, this should happen simultaneously.

This inside and outside does not only apply to the individual human being and his internal and external world. In ever-increasing circles it applies equally to every form of human community, e.g. marriage, the family, the group, right up to the whole of society and finally to humanity and the whole of creation.

Crucially important, besides the individual as the starting point for change, is the group or, better said, the cohesive solidarity community that, in networking with others, can become an essential building block of the contemporary "People of God".

Change is thus to be striven for not primarily with other people and those "above" but with oneself and in the closer association of solidarity. This is in accordance with Martin Buber's insight, "The Archimedean point for changing the world is changing oneself."

Indeed, if the goal of life is above all for man to experience the meaning of his existence and to try to live according to his destiny, then it is crucial for the change and maturation process that comes with it that he learns and practices to think and act responsibly, both alone and in association with more or less like-minded people. When it comes to the person himself and his career, it is a hindrance and not beneficial to shift responsibility "upwards" and thereby promote irresponsibility and a sense of entitlement. Man then remains a subject and dependent, losing his dignity, his path of maturation and his image of God.

Every self has an inside and an outside. The inside corresponds to the soul and the spirit, the outside to the body. The interior hangs on an umbilical cord to the transpersonal, to the transcendent, to the divine, just as the ego extends from the small mind-ego to the depth of the being. However, inside and outside also stand for the ancient pairs of terms "praying and working" and "faith and works", as well as for the basic concepts of the participatory management theory "cohesion and locomotion". Here, "cohesion" stands for all efforts towards interior cohesion and "locomotion" for all purposeful external activity. Both aspects are equally valid and important for the individual and for each group.

The participatory management theory points out that equal attention must be paid to both of these priorities. Where cohesion is neglected, i.e. where all energy flows into locomotion, disintegration occurs relatively quickly, breaking apart. In the heyday of the peace movement, there were many examples of such a mistaken attitude. The overemphasis on cohesion is just as damaging. The movement solidifies and degenerates into a drinking club and a hen party. Everything centers around itself.

In the same way as "cohesion and locomotion", the other pairs of terms apply to each "we" as well as to the ego. As is well known, there is such a thing as a group soul and a group spirit. "Team spirit" is a common term for it. This common interior also manifests itself as a common exterior, even if this is only for a limited time, for example for the duration of participation in an event. The common exterior, the external identity, becomes particularly clear when uniforms are worn. This is not only the case with sports and the military but also, for example, with teenage gangs, soccer fans, rockers and the like.

Hugh J. Schonfield[43] writes that the most primitive form of group and community building takes place through the definition of opponents and enemies. If this is becoming increasingly difficult at the military level in Europe in view of the developments in Eastern Europe. It is all the more evident at the economic level, where the competition, which, according to an idiotic catchphrase, never sleeps, must always serve as an enemy image to justify everything possible and impossible. The more and more emerging xenophobia pursues similar aims.

C. G. Jung finds a neutral approach, speaking of a common myth, such as a religious conviction, as the basis for group formation. Such a myth can, if it stands at a high level, get along without opponents and enemy figures. However, even the religions in their everyday reality rarely or hardly manage without this primitive tool. Yes, even the phrase "And deliver us from evil" from the Lord's Prayer is, for a superficial

43 English historian of Jewish origin, who is best known in the English speaking world for his books on the origins of Christianity.

Christianity, an alibi for a primitive dualism that makes it easier to pin down what is different as the incarnation of evil and, if necessary, to fight it with all means.

Real life and a healthy development manifests itself through a balanced field of tension in the two polarities described, i.e. between the two pole pairs I and Thou on the one hand and internal and external on the other. Connected with this is an oscillation of the respective priorities, from the I to the Thou, from the internal to the external and vice versa.

If we evaluate our past actions and activities based on this insight, we notice that they mostly had the change of others, i.e. the Thou, and the change of the external, e.g. disarmament, as their goal. However, to stay with the example, the external disarmament presupposes an internal disarmament. This has to start firstly with ourselves. That every contamination and destruction of the external world corresponds to a contamination and destruction of the internal world has been and is often enough overlooked.

Every activity must not only start with myself. It must always see the change of myself as its focus and its real field of action. This approach becomes all the more important the more we realize that every person who meets me is holding up a mirror to me, so to speak. When I get upset about him and his way of acting, I usually get angry about my own painful experiences and my own less gratifying traits. This insight should above all induce me to pursue the causes within myself and to seek and conduct a conversation with the other person from this focal point.

As far as this criticism is true, it is not surprising that these efforts have often come to nothing. Two examples may stand for a holistic approach in this sense:

The "Silence for Peace" action on late Friday afternoons. Unfortunately, it has fallen asleep in most places. Probably mainly because we are not aware of the holistic meaning of this action and also the psycho-hygienic importance of perseverance and a steady temporal order. Silence for Peace is in fact something like a demonstrative meditation anchored to a fixed point in time and thus regularly recurring. It can also be a meditative demonstration or, even better, an admonitory meditation. It aims at both internal and external effects, both for those who stand there in silence and for those who see them standing there.

The second example is of a similar nature:

At the annual meeting of the Fellowship of Reconciliation mentioned at the beginning of this article, as a reaction to the Chernobyl catastrophe, it was also proposed to introduce and maintain a "power pause" by switching off the electricity consumers in our apartment on Friday evening, approximately between 8 and 9 p.m. In contrast to spectacular, demonstrative actions, which cannot be sustained in the long run, this is a silent demonstrative act that only affects those who practice it and those who come to the apartment at the right time, either by invitation or by chance.

Both forms of action aim, in relation to our network of relationships outlined above, in all four directions, i.e. inwards and outwards on the one hand, and on the other hand at the I and Thou. They thus have a better chance of lasting and profound change, albeit in tiny steps. They therefore resemble water, which, as is well known, even hollows out the stone drop by drop.

The two polarities between the internal and the external on the one hand and between the I and Thou on the other are overlaid by the polarity between right and wrong, good and evil, salvation and disaster. The following basic concepts for a responsible life and our desirable reaction to them can be introduced:

We should learn, live, love and let (grow) the right, the good and the salutary. On the other hand, the wrong, the evil and harm should be made apparent, ascertained, addressed and accepted.

The four "L" on the positive side are opposite four "A" on the negative side. They correspond—more or less—in pairs.

At first this sounds suspiciously like the mnemonic tricks of a head teacher pointing with his forefinger. But if we understand the life of the individual and the closer solidarity community as a process of learning, practicing and maturing, then such aids will gain in importance.

Just as it is a matter of learning what is right, so it is "necessary" to uncover injustice—to make it really apparent. The learning process on this level fertilizes both. To the same extent that I learn what is wrong, for example in our economy and in dealing with money, I learn almost simultaneously what is right, and vice versa.

Once the injustice has been revealed, it is important to look at it, to confront reality—however horrible it may be. Neither the escape from reality nor its repression solves problems—neither my own nor those of others or of society as a whole. This is very difficult, because it opens the gates of hell and opens our eyes to Auschwitz and Hiroshima, to the mercilessly competitive society, to the murderous plundering of the technically underdeveloped countries. But it also opens our eyes to the deeper layers of the soul—our own and those of others—in which all our greatness and meanness are rooted. This is only bearable if the opposite pole of living together positively and in solidarity, at least on a small scale, is not neglected. This, in turn, requires that the spiritual depths of the inner being be tapped and used as a source of strength both on the level of the individual person and on the next higher level, the closer community.

At this level, it is a matter of serving the truth, of looking at the sinister reality, of perceiving it and of preparing a place for the salutary alternative with one's own life, individually and collectively.

To accept the ominous reality as such is no less difficult—whether with me or with others. As we know from psychology, the defensive struggle only leads us deeper and deeper into the entanglement. Love is the secret recipe, love for oneself and for others.

This love, however, does not mean that we should cover everything with a cloak of silence. That only conceals and does not heal. The disaster continues to proliferate. Max Frisch writes about this:[44]

"One is silent and feels Christian by enjoying one's own mercy, a kind of mercy that changes nothing. The mere renunciation of the risk of judgment is not yet

44 From: Tagebuch 1946-49, Suhrkamp, Frankfurt

justice, let alone goodness or even love. It is simply non-binding, nothing more. But it is precisely this non-committal, the silence on an atrocity that is known, that is probably the most common kind of our complicity".

The Bible is of a similar opinion. In chapter 33 of the book of Ezekiel it says:

> "When I say unto the wicked, O wicked man, thou shalt surely die; if thou dost not speak to warn the wicked from his way, that wicked man shall die in his iniquity; but his blood will I require at thine hand."

This does not mean that we should all presume the role of prophets with a divine mandate. The duty of critical dialogue, which also calls into question our own convictions, is unavoidable, because in the warning lies the possibility of salvation. The story of Jonah makes this clear in a positive way for Nineveh. Whereas Jesus' warning went unheard, the story ended negatively for Jerusalem and all Israel, namely with annihilation. The same applies, incidentally, to Jesus' warning and what was made of it in Christianity.

It is therefore necessary to start a dialogue with the disaster in spite of all the tensions of pain and suffering and to deal with it. This can be a long process and unsuccessful. However, this possibility must be reckoned with.

After all, we cannot expect a NATO Secretary General to become Mahatma Gandhi overnight. The tragedy of such short-term and superficially unsolvable situations must be endured. We have to realize that the essential, the decisive, is not feasible but must evolve. This understanding can only be endured without great emotional damage through serenity, which ultimately arises from love. Hanspeter Padrutt writes on the subject:

And he lets it happen,
Everything as it will...

from the Song of the Hurdy Gurdy Man from the song cycle "Die Winterreise"[45] (The Winter Journey by Franz Schubert) from a revolution from wanting to let go, from arbitrary wanting to serenity, which is no indifferent laissez-faire but a loving laissez-etre[46]. From wanting of the will to power to a surrender that lies beyond activity and passivity, beyond a violent domination as well as a powerless ability to let things drift".

Just as God makes the sun rise and rain fall upon the just and the unjust, so we must stand up to such situations in living tension, even if it is easier said than done. There is the danger that the tension rises too much and discharges in a short-circuit, i.e. actions of coercion and violence. This is just as great as the temptation to break off the dialogue and to demonize the respective other(s), i.e. to make them the scapegoat, and in this way to succumb even to a primitive dualism. The third aberration lies in the attempt to degrade the "unteachable" Other from the Thou to the It, reducing it on the path of power from an independent subject to a manipulable object. Other forms of

45 Padrutt, Der epochale Winter, Zürich, 1984.

46 This can best be translated this way: From a making and letting go to a being and letting grow.

aberration would be the flight into helpless resignation or even being overwhelmed by despair and depression.

We lie to ourselves with the statement, "Here good—there evil". No matter on what level we do this, whether on the lowest level of the I and Thou or on a higher plain, for instance with the West as We and the East or the South as the Other. Each one of us lives himself, so to speak, in a mixture of wrong and right, of disaster and salvation. Thus the border does not run between the I and the We on the one hand and any one else on the other hand. It runs right through all of us. Yes, in the end it is not a border at all but rather a merging of the most diverse shades that coexist with one another. This is also something that has to be accepted and endured.

If we look at historical development, we can see that man has progressively learned to extend the circles in which he can get along without military enemies. In historical dimensions, it is not so long ago that the Free Imperial Cities of Rottweil and Villingen[47] waged war against each other, and France as "hereditary enemy" is still a gruesome but tangible memory for many living contemporary witnesses. Today, even our "hawks" are struggling to apostrophize the Soviet Union as the empire of evil and it is becoming increasingly difficult for them. In order to be able to hold on to their enmity thinking, they direct their gaze more and more towards the south, as the Gulf War demonstrated in a terrible way. But this behavior is becoming more and more difficult to communicate to a critical

47 Small cities in southwestern Germany. (S.E.)

public. Fortunately, a positive development can be seen. Its goal is to grow beyond the idea of antagonism and enmity and to recognize man and nature as one big community. At the same time, the opposites are not eliminated. We will rather learn to live with them, even if the resulting tensions should be painful. Isaiah says this in visionary terms:

The wolf also shall dwell with the lamb,
and the leopard shall lie down with the kid;
and the calf and the young lion
and the fatling together;
and a little child shall lead them.
And the cow and the bear shall feed;
their young ones shall lie down together:
and the lion shall eat straw like the ox.

Freedom and Security

About new social structures

The industrialization of the past two centuries has also brought about enormous changes in the social sphere. The outdated structures have increasingly broken down. The extended family of the former agrarian society has dissolved. Today even the nuclear family has become a temporary association. Not only has the divorce rate increased dramatically but also the number of so-called "singles", i.e. people living alone, has risen dramatically. Even in my rural hometown, it grew by more than 60% between the last two censuses. The divorce rate, like the growing number of single parents, shows that even for children, the family is no longer the basic social structure that is taken for granted. The development shows a progressive atomization of society, in which the individual, economically secured against all dangers but without the security of human community, is increasingly isolated and lonely.

After decades of great suffering for the working classes, the social legislation introduced in Germany by Bismarck has taken away the greatest financial hardships from this development. But it has also encouraged social fragmentation. Whereas in the past almost everyone was economically dependent on their family, clan and community and thus also dependent on them, financial security through compulsory insurance has eliminated the greatest risks of illness and old age and made people financially independent to a large extent. Previously, economic security and welfare could be found at the price of submission to the constraints of mostly patriarchal family structures.

This development is not unwelcome in industry but also in the world of economic policy. Quite the contrary in fact. The mobile individual, young, "dynamic" and capable of high performance, is sought, demanded and supported. It represents the social ideal that is presented to us in advertising everywhere. The social and psychological problems almost inevitably associated with it are often enough overlooked. In any case, they play only a subordinate role in our political thinking, for which a kind of repair system usually seems to be sufficient. For decades, it was believed that these problems could be solved primarily through professionalization and specialization. The growing number and variety of social professions and social institutions bear witness to this.

Increasingly, however, the realization is dawning that two major deficits remain in this approach.

On the one hand, the professionalization of all necessary social services cannot be paid for. It is irrelevant whether these are provided by public institutions, such as municipal hospitals and nursing homes for the elderly, or on a private basis. If today a place in a nursing home for the elderly costs 3000 Marks and more per month despite an understaffed and badly paid nursing service, then it becomes obvious that it is impossible for all old people in need of care will be able to afford this. They have neither enough money for it themselves, nor is society prepared to provide the necessary funds for it in the public budgets. The time is foreseeable when the municipalities will no longer have enough funds for their growing social spending. This problem cannot be fundamentally solved even by means of long-term care insurance, however necessary it may be.

On the other hand, it is becoming apparent that professional care and financial security are indispensable, but that the psychological and emotional needs of people for care, love and security in familial structures are usually not adequately met. This already seems to be a problem of relative numbers. A physically and/or psychologically "needy person" is more likely to find fulfillment in all his or her needs within a group of "helpers" than in the reverse relationship with many "needy persons" and relatively few "helpers" even if some are "laymen" and others "professionals". Moreover, in a relatively "healthy" environment, it is more likely to become clear to the "needy" that they must ultimately take the decisive steps on their path to solving the problem themselves.

The inverse numerical ratio, which is ultimately unhealthy for both sides, remains an essential basic element in almost all full-professional social institutions if the costs are not to explode into the abyss, not to mention the limits of resilience in the nursing professions. The tendency of today's citizens to evade their natural social obligations to relatives in need of help as far as possible in their private lives will eventually strike back at them. They themselves will be abandoned when they need help at some point.

I know of a family with a farming sideline in which a mentally handicapped adult son works. He finds meaning and fulfillment there and is guided and accompanied by his family members in a friendly and loving way. If the house and farm have to be dissolved after the death of the father, the only option left for the handicapped son is the confined institution. Such an accommodation does not only cost the society a lot of money. It also means for the person concerned that he is confined and withers in a foreign environment. In any case, this is usually the case if he has spent most of his life differently. The gratifying alternative, which is still in existence, only works because the family members themselves take responsibility for the weaker member of their circle and exercise it to the benefit of all.

The development described above makes it clear that the process of reducing the size of families and isolating people only functions at best inadequately and unsatisfactorily. Even this is only possible if society at large, i.e. at least at the municipal level, ensures that all those who for whatever reason cannot withstand this process of isolation are taken in and cared for in some kind of collective professional-specialized social institution. Conversely, small families for a limited period of time and those living alone "function" satisfactorily as producers (with the associated professional activity). They play the optimal roles for the economy and for man's urge for freedom and development as producers and consumers only as long as everyone is healthy and capable of high performance. As soon as small children, the sick, the less able and the elderly are added, this system no longer functions. And since almost all of us become ill, underperforming and old at some point in our lives—not to mention the inevitable childhood—we are all confronted with this gap. We only repress it as best we can and for as long as we can.

What are the alternatives to this aberration?

There is no going back to the old social structures. Even the path of return to the extended and permanent family, as propagated by the churches, is only feasible in isolated cases. However, it offers no solution for society as a whole. In the old structures, as already mentioned, security and safety had to be bought at the price of subjugation and conformity. This price is—correctly—no longer paid today by the majority of people striving for freedom and independence. Even in societies like the Japanese, where the old social structures are still particularly strong today, the upheaval is becoming noticeable. The rebellion against the old structures, which has been largely suppressed to date, is leading there, for example, to an above-average number of health problems in the stomach, liver and bile areas, which is largely due to this situation.

Even the old communal structures, such as monastic orders and other forms of similar communities, show signs of decay that make the same thing clear. At least in all those cases in which the longing for freedom and the desire for independence is massively suppressed.

The largely closed circle of these traditional forms of community with submission to a leader and dogmatic norms of behavior with exclusion of outsiders and rebels is obsolete as a social structure for our pluralistic times. The search for new social structures is therefore probably more about open systems—graphically speaking, the open spiral instead of the closed circle.

Beyond that—and this seems to me to be decisive—it is about freedom and security as the two decisive antipoles in the objectives of new communities. These are terms I first heard from Heinrich Spaemann[48] and later read in the childhood memories of Astrid Lindgren. Until now, the combination of both terms as a demand seemed to us to be realizable only in community for a limited time. In any case, our social structures show this very clearly from the short-term communities in courses, seminars, the associations and action groups for special objectives as well as the temporary marriages and families. However, it is about community in the long run!

We all need economic security and emotional support, not just in the short term but in the long term. That is the one pole. But it must—and therein lies our challenge today—be united in living tension with its counterpart, namely freedom and independence. This sounds like the demand of squaring the circle and yet this is the central concern in every human relationship, be it a friendship, a marriage or a family. The development of the individual human being, the individuation as C. G. Jung called it, is indispensable. But this self-re-

48 Heinrich Spaemann (* July 15, 1903 in Sölde; † May 1, 2001 in Überlingen) was a German Roman Catholic priest and writer.

alization, as it is often called, is inevitably doomed to failure, both individually-psychically and collectively-socially, if it is pursued alone or even at the expense of fellow human beings. It can only progress in living community with others, that is, on the path of socialization. Individuation and socialization are thus in the same polar relationship of tension as freedom and security.

It goes without saying that crises, misunderstandings and conflicts occur. Therefore, it is also necessary to develop, learn and practice methods and procedures that enable us to perceive, accept and deal with these not only on a factual level, i.e. logically-rational-analytically, but also in the emotional area. I myself have learned a lot in the latter area in particular—an area that is usually regarded as childish or feminine and neglected—and have taken great steps on the path to personal development and maturation. Elisabeth (Beth) Weiner[49], the great German-American therapist, who became known in Europe primarily through her

49 Beth Weiner was born in 1924 as Elisabeth Wolff in Neustadt an der Weinstrasse Germany into a middle-class and wealthy Jewish family. "My father was a respected citizen who knew practically everyone in town". When Hitler came to power the child Beth was nine years old. Her father and her brother were interned for a short time in the Dachau concentration camp. At the age of 12 she fled, partly separated from her family, first to Holland and in 1940 via England to the USA. Her famous book is called "Wo Leben ist, ist Hoffnung" (Where there's Life there's Hope). (http://www.akdh.ch/bethweiner.htm – translated).

collaboration with Elisabeth Kübler-Ross[50], was very helpful to me in this process.

The "unfinished business", as Kübler-Ross calls it, not only prevents us from a peaceful and dignified death. The suppressed feelings such as anger, sadness, fear, etc. —and that is what these unfinished business deals prove to be in most cases—are not only driving forces in the search for new social structures. Often enough, they also prove to be stumbling blocks in their realization. As a result, many attempts, especially in the communal sector—we think only of shared housing—often fail early.

In the quest for freedom and independence it is often overlooked that this is complementary to the longing for security. In the search for security, however, the insight that this also has a transcendental component is often neglected. It is always also a longing for God, for the protection of God. Martin Buber once wrote that the longing for God is the longing for community and the longing for community is the longing for God. Both are mutually dependent. That is important to know, because no human being and no human community can satisfy the deepest longing of man. It is the longing for safety in God, for unity with God. This unity was lost with creation or with the expulsion from paradise or with the exodus of the "prodigal son". Just

50 Elisabeth Kübler-Ross (July 8, 1926 – August 24, 2004) was a Swiss-American psychiatrist, a pioneer in near-death studies, and author of the internationally best-selling book, On Death and Dying (1969), where she first discussed her theory of the five stages of grief, also known as the "Kübler-Ross model".

as the child is released—must be released—from unity with its mother.

The aspect of security among people is about a supportive, cohesive community that offers not only economic security but also warm and critical loving acceptance and attention. The latter is usually not possible without the courage to work through one's own deficits and the conflicts that arise from them.

I am convinced that the formation and preservation of community continues to require that social responsibility is seen beyond the community members and that consequences are drawn from this. In the open systems of new communities, the physically, mentally and socially weaker, the marginalized and the underprivileged have a firm place. The "sick" are just as important as anything else for the health and internal and external growth of the community. One of the Bodelschwingh women in Bethel[51] once said that children, the sick and animals are indispensable to any community. This is without doubt true. It is precisely the pathological, progressive process of division that can be observed in our high-performance society and that, as in high-performance sports, increasingly and visibly separates the victorious elite from the rest of society. This requires a counter-movement—for the good and for the benefit of society.

51 Healthy or ill, disabled or not—in Bethel we are convinced that all people in their diversity can naturally live, learn and work together. For 150 years the v. Bodelschwinghschen Stiftungen Bethel have been committed to helping all those who are in need of help, support or assistance. (https://www.bethel.de/ueber-uns.html – translated).

Consequently, the social task also becomes a political one—the close level at which responsibility must be seen and acted upon. This political responsibility extends beyond the social sector. The social life of such communities inevitably raises economic issues and forces their resolution. They range from the question of employment, income generation and distribution to the production of goods and the importance of money and interest. Thus, in a living process, many areas of human coexistence are made tangible and perceptible through discussion, learning, practice and teaching in the best sense of the word.

The basis for this process and the communities that emerge and grow in the process is the search for a common myth, as C. G. Jung calls it. It is well known that the most primitive form of community building takes place when the group determines the common opponents or even enemies. The confrontation with them, the fight against them, provides the binding agent for community building. In contrast to this destructive bond, real community grows with the shared myth. It is all the more lasting the deeper this myth is rooted in the transcendent, in the spiritual or religious. The further back this historical continuity goes, the more it is able to form a new living vision out of both.

For me, this is a myth that ties in with Judeo-Christian traditions and, in the sense of the idea of God's people, aims at the emergence of communities as nodes of a worldwide network in the sense of a pioneering society for all of humanity[52]. Certainly such a

52 cf. Haller, Die heilsame Alternative, Wuppertal 1989.

myth can have other roots. For me, however, spiritual depth and the renunciation of power, domination and violence seem indispensable. Whether these constraints are to be evaluated absolutely, I am not able to say.

The foundation of a healthy society in our time is formed by elective affinities with a common myth. These are new social structures with communities that are open dynamic systems in the long term, trying to offer their members freedom and security. They remain viable and become more and more alive when they take on and try to live up to their social responsibility beyond an inward focus with its danger of selfish self-interest. This social responsibility leads logically and necessarily to political responsibility and political work. The meaning and purpose of these new structures are thereby enhanced and can thus become salutary experiences.

Every week, millions of German citizens feverishly await the drawing of the lottery or place their hopes in other forms of gambling. Predominantly, these are people who have neither hope nor the prospect of making big money by working. Even if their income is sufficient to secure their livelihood, there is still a great desire to be able to afford not only a roof over their heads but also one or two luxuries through winning at gambling. Even those who pursue a professional career have the same goal, besides the desire for success and prestige.

Generally speaking, we try to achieve the largest possible surplus of money. This is the difference between the income from our own gainful employment and other, ultimately unproductive income such as interest and return on capital, inheritance, gambling, speculation and other forms of robbery and theft on the one hand and the cost of our livelihood on the other. Nearly everyone tries to sell their own performance as expensively as possible and to cover their own needs as cheaply as possible in order to achieve such surpluses. This way of thinking and acting is regarded as one of the central characteristics of the free market economy.

Such surpluses could and would be invested profitably (in other words, with unproductive multiplication), serve luxury consumption or create material securities such as one's own four walls. The dream for many would be to be released from the obligation this way from the necessity for permanent gainful employment. This would mean to be freed from all the burdens and uncertainties associated with it, and to let the money—that is, other people—work for them.

What applies to individuals applies equally to all commercial enterprises. The striving for surpluses as the difference between income and expenditure, between earnings and outgoings, is, however, identified here by its own terminology. We speak in all openness and honesty of profit maximization as the central goal of business.

So it is not that the main task of the economy is to meet the material needs of man. These are only of interest insofar as they are connected with purchasing power and promise to make a contribution to the described goal. Even existentially indispensable basic needs without purchasing power mobilize nobody in the economy. Purchasing power is what attracts the economy. This goes so far that, if purchasing power is available, even needs are artificially awakened and promoted in order to create new markets and absorb such purchasing power.

And how is purchasing power generated? Purchasing power is generated by revenues from an offer of goods or services for which there are buyers on the market who take advantage of this offer and pay money for it. A supply of services without buyers, i.e. without demand with purchasing power, comes up against a void. But whether someone becomes rich or poor even with a successful offer does not necessarily depend on his work performance but on the relation of his offer together with that of his competitors to the total demand. As is well known, according to the famous principle of the free market economy, supply and demand regulate the level of the price. An excess of supply leads to falling prices. An excess of demand drives them upwards. This basic law is practically always valid, as long as it is not overruled by cartel-like collusion ranging from price monopolies to collective agreements.

In the search for promising offers that offer the prospect of surpluses, both the individual in his or her choice of career and the entrepreneur in his or her choice of product have the following range of options: Type of service, quantity of service, quality of service, time of service, place of service, membership of a race or a social group.

Whether a person becomes an unskilled worker or an electronics engineer, or whether the company produces simple stamped parts or computer-controlled machine tools, this has a significant impact on the chances of success in terms of maximizing profits. Furthermore, whether the person works part-time or only produces small quantities due to low productivity is equally important. The same applies to the quality of performance, both for the individual employee and for each company. Surprisingly, the time and place of performance are also of considerable influence. The first to bring strawberries or a new product to market will earn more than the latecomer. And whether he works as a mechanic or a retailer in the Stuttgart or Zurich area, or as a black man in the bush somewhere in West Africa, his income is influenced quite considerably.

The same spectrum of possibilities is of course also available on the demand side. This means that the desired surplus can be achieved not only on the supply side but also on the demand side, provided that basic needs are covered first. The old Adam Smith, the foster father of all liberal economists, put this in a nutshell by saying that diligence (on the supply side) and thrift (on the demand side) automatically lead to prosperity. However, this is only partly true, because if everyone were both diligent in the sense of increasing production volumes and thrifty in the sense of restricting consumption, there would inevitably be a surplus of supply, which would inhibit sales and depress prices. Only if diligence is practiced by individuals and small groups and if it is to be understood in the application of creative spirit to increase productivity, does prosperity grow. This is because the effort required to produce the service to be offered, for example in the form of unit costs, decreases.

The fact that the translation of creative spirit and new ideas into material reality requires capital is only mentioned in passing. Nevertheless, it is of crucial importance. The consequence of this is that those who themselves have the necessary capital or have access to sources of capital are at an advantage over the others because they can actually implement performance-enhancing ideas. The others, in contrast, have to do without it often enough due to lack of capital[53]. Since capital is more likely to be offered for reasons of security and secure interest to the performance elite than to the so-called under-performers, the flow of capital reinforces the vicious circle that already begins with pricing at the expense of the (industrially) weaker performers.

The generation of freely available surpluses, the maximization of profits, is for most people the central goal of all economic activity. In order to achieve this goal, private companies try more or less systematically. In the business world, however, they try extremely systematically and with great expertise and dedication to turn the screws of the described spectrum of possibilities on both the supply and the demand side in order to achieve the greatest possible surpluses. Great efforts are being made with growing pressure to perform in order to improve the nature, quantity, quality, time and place of one's own performance on the supply side.

53 For more details on the money problem see Haller, Die heilsame Alternative, Wuppertal 1989.

This is to avoid slipping into market areas with excess supply and poor prices, or to try to push through from such areas to the top of the performance elite with good prices. In the same way, on the demand side, massive pressure is exerted on suppliers to improve their performance while prices tend to fall. To this end, attempts are being made to expand the number of suppliers in order to achieve a supply overhang with falling prices. On the world markets for raw materials, this has been achieved in recent years with great success for buyers in the industrialized nations. This has been demonstrated by the fact that raw material prices have generally been falling for years. This development can be fatal for the supplier if he has no freedom of choice in his offer, neither in the choice of the products to be offered nor in the fundamental question of participation in the market. Then he becomes a slave to the market and its customers and often a victim of them. We find this situation today especially in the countries of the so-called Third World, which are forced by the duties of debt service to participate in world trade on conditions that are often murderous for them.

The race for the better positions is taking on a hectic pace in the Western European countries on their way to the domestic market. Everyone knows that "the early bird catches the worm". Not only for the future European domestic market is the wrangling for the best starting positions intense, also the efforts in the Eastern European countries are aimed at getting out of the role of suppliers of cheap raw materials and cheap, unbranded finished products and buyers of expensive high-tech products on the world market. This role, as the North-South divide shows, does not bring the desired surpluses, but is actually almost always in deficit. To pay for relatively few high-tech products and high-tech know-how, enormous quantities of raw materials have to be supplied, as the following example from an individual perspective demonstrates:

A graduate of a college for electronic engineers in hardware and software earns between 4000 and 5000 DM per month (1991). If a chicken farmer wants to save personnel costs in his "production", i.e. employ fewer people, he can now automate the lighting, air conditioning, feeding, egg and manure removal by using an appropriately programmed process computer (of course connected with suitable auxiliary equipment). As far as the necessary programs are not available as standard, a software company will offer him the monthly output of the engineer described at the beginning of this article for at least 20,000 DM for the development of the corresponding program modules, later charging him. A "man-month", as the technical term is called, thus costs at least 20,000 DM for programming. The chicken farmer can pay for such a service only with the products of his chickens, i.e. their eggs. For 20.000 DM, 200.000 eggs have to be delivered—roughly speaking. This corresponds—always in approximate numbers—to the laying performance of 10,000 hens. 10,000 chickens are able to produce a monthly output that has a comparable market value to that of a software engineer.

Thus our dilemma becomes obvious. The economic performance of one software engineer has a market value like that of 10.000 chickens... or 5 to 10 Poles or 10 to 100 Indians in South America.

Given this insanity, it is no wonder that everything is being done everywhere to be considered to the software engineers rather than to the chickens (or Poles or Indios).

The best prospects in this hunt for profit maximization are obviously the financially strong suppliers of high-tech products who act as buyers of raw materials. Their supply is rewarded with high prices and their demand is met at low cost to them. They therefore make good profits. The balance of trade surpluses of the Federal Republic of Germany or Japan speak for themselves. No wonder that the battle for the top positions is getting harder and harder, since everyone—whether as an individual, as a company or as a nation state—wants to be among those who are up front and can make money.

The fact that those in the worse starting position have to get increasingly into debt in their ultimately almost hopeless effort not to miss the connection makes things even worse. Not only do they earn far less for their services than the high-tech industrial nations, their revenues are also capped by interest and redemption charges. Thus the vicious circle of growing impoverishment can hardly be broken. The payment obligations from debt burdens also no longer allow an exit from such unequal business relationships. This debt bondage becomes a modern form of slavery.

The Brazilian labor leader Luis Ignacio Silva writes[54]:

54 Quoted from Susan George, Sie sterben an unserem Geld,

"The Third World War has already begun—a silent but therefore no less sinister war. Instead of soldiers, children have to lose their lives. Instead of millions of wounded, there are millions of unemployed. Instead of bridges being destroyed, factories, schools, hospitals and entire economies are being destroyed. It is a war against the Latin American continent and against the entire Third World, a war for foreign debt. Its sharpest weapon is the interest rate and it is more deadly than the atomic bomb".

When some time ago the Prime Minister of Poland undertook a kind of goodwill tour in the Federal Republic of Germany to relieve the distress in Poland, every expert knew that this was practically an attempt at a lost cause. They are encumbered by billions of dollars in foreign debts and the resulting interest and repayment burdens. In view of the fact that the Polish supply of agricultural products, raw materials and cheap industrial goods is located in market areas with excess supply and miserable prices, an improvement of the economic situation in Poland cannot really be expected. If imports were not curtailed at the expense of improving the efficiency of the economy and exports increased through even more radical consumption restraint, the balance of trade and payments would remain in deficit. Any child can understand this. And yet our media during the Polish state visit pretended that the improvement of the economic situation in Poland was a realistic possibility.

rororo aktuell, Hamburg 1988.

The "sacred cow" of the free market economy that we are all so fond of cannot solve the problems of inequality on either a national or global scale. On the contrary, it exacerbates them. This cannot be made clear enough. Admittedly, the public debate about the weaknesses of our system is not exactly popular today. The obvious bankruptcy of state capitalism and the planned economy of the Eastern European countries and the bankruptcy of the trade union "public economy" visible in the fate of the *Neue Heimat*, the *Coop*, the *Bank für Gemeinwirtschaft* and *Volksfürsorge*, have indeed caused sustained cries of triumph from the market economy agents. And yet all this can neither conceal nor dispel the facts described.

In the military sector, the term "security partnership" has been used in recent years to successfully challenge traditional strategies, at least in the East-West conflict. Thus, consideration for the vital interests of the potential adversary (even if, as in the case of security needs, they are purely subjective in nature) has been recognized as an important element of any military security policy. The first disarmament successes are proof of this. The discussion about renouncing the ability to wage offensive war and focusing on concepts of strictly defensive warfare is also capable of gradually softening the fronts and—it is to be hoped—gradually reducing the massive threat to humans and nature. A comparable discussion has so far been lacking in the economic field, although it is obvious that military imperialism has long since been replaced by economic imperialism, at least among the industrialized nations. Significantly, the great victors of the last world war were the last to understand this. The Soviet Union, like the United States, armed itself almost to death. Both countries have degenerated into industrial weaklings, while the two main losers of that war, Germany and Japan, are the victors in today's economic imperialism. In this respect, our German army and NATO with their present concepts have long since degenerated into an anachronism, even if the pigheaded individuals are far from understanding this. They remain the eternal yesterday and will probably only discover tomorrow what today was.

The task of the hour is to conduct a critical dialogue with and about economic imperialism. We must ask publicly what the analogous term for the world economy to "security partnership" should be. We must also ask what a competitive partnership might look like. We must question publicly what "consideration for the vital interests of the potential adversary"—in the economy, that is the supplier, the competitor and the customer, but also the so-called employee—should look like in practice.

This considerateness has a good tradition that is deliberately hardly noticed. The haggling prior to a price agreement is still widespread today, especially in southern countries. Originally, the main purpose of haggling was to disclose the economic situation of both partners and to get to know each other so that a price appropriate to this situation could be agreed upon for the business sought by both sides. Of course, in most cases this concern has been lost but this old tradition could be continued in the search for new, modern methods without giving up the idea of a free economy.

In haggling we do have a free market economy system. However, price formation is not primarily based on the law of supply and demand. Rather, it is primarily based on the economic situation of the two negotiating partners. Of course, it takes into account the limits of both sides' ability to compromise.

Discussion of these questions must become an essential concern in the continuation of the conciliar process if justice in the biblical scope of the term is to be increasingly satisfied.

The Challenge of the Global Debt Crisis

As everyone knows in the meantime, the mountain of debt and with it the economic misery of the so-called Third World is growing seemingly inexorably from year to year. The banking world is not in a position to find and go any real way out beyond securing its own interests. And so one debt rescheduling agreement follows another without seriously improving the situation. Rather, the epidemic is beginning to spread more and more from the so-called Third World to Eastern Europe and into the rich countries, where the same, ultimately failed concepts are being used to finance development and growth.

What does all this concern us?

To clarify this question, it is first of all important to know that apart from the causes of mismanagement that the arms mania and capital flight for which the debtor countries themselves are responsible are the main reasons for the progressive impoverishment in our system of price formation and the compulsion to pay interest and compound interest. In pricing, bad prices lead to insufficient income. The poor prices are mostly caused by supply overhangs. These in turn are often caused by the obligations of the debt service. In concrete terms, this means that in order to meet their financial obligations, debtor countries have to make huge offers on the world markets. This inevitably puts pressure on prices when demand is comparatively lower. The situation is aggravated by the fact that the low income that can be obtained is often insufficient to meet the obligations of the debt service. This is all the more so when the debt service explodes into infinity due to high interest rates and compound interest in an exponential development.

The disease can therefore only be combated at its root. We must not only rely on the laws of the free market when setting prices but also learn to take into account the vital interests of our trading partners. In concrete terms, this means that we do not lust for minimum prices on the market but pay sufficient prices to ensure the humane existence of the supplier and an adequate economic development.

As already described, this way of thinking has long since found its place in military doctrine under the concept of security partnership, at least for East-West relations. In the economic sphere, it has not even been seriously discussed as a theory. A church that takes the conciliar process seriously and thus also the concern for justice could and should be the initiator and place for this discussion. It should also promote the realization of this approach through the at least partially already existing Third World networks.

The situation is actually even clearer when it comes to the question of interest. In the Mosaic legislation the taking of interest within the national community is simply forbidden[55]. It is only permissible for those who do not belong to the national community. This view is obviously intensified in biblical history. In any case, in Ezekiel, the death sentence is already imposed on every interest taker[56]. The basic biblical attitude is initially also adopted by the church, as the statements of the various councils up to the late Middle Ages make clear. Luther was also quite clear in his statements on this issue. For example, he once described the usurer as a "werewolf, worse even than all tyrants, murderers and robbers, almost as evil as the devil himself."[57]

A dramatic change can only be observed in the past two centuries, when the demands of the economy for free, interest-bearing (and morally unobjectionable) money markets to finance the growing capital requirements of industrialization were reflected in a reversal of the church's attitude to the question of interest. One of the decisive tricks that facilitated this about-turn, especially for the inexperienced layman, was the distinction between reprehensible usury and Godly interest. However, no one can seriously draw a proper line between the two, especially since even a relatively low interest rate can lead to an exponential, i.e. explosive, increase in debt and thus become murderous. This always occurs when the debt service consisting of interest and repayment cannot be performed at all or only partially without great sacrifice. Then even the

55 e.g. Exodus 22, 24 ff.

56 Ezekiel 18, 13.

57 Quoted from "Zeitschrift für Sozialökonomie" 80/89

relatively low interest rate becomes usury in almost every emergency. It then becomes liable to interest in whole or in part. The exponential development takes its course with all its murderous consequences.

Quite apart from this, it must be pointed out again and again that the interest payment per se ultimately represents an unproductive income and, together with the compound interest effect, leads to an irresponsible, even murderous skimming off of income and a shift of purchasing power from the poor to the rich. As the following diagram shows, this law is mathematically so clear and practically-economically so emphatic that it is astonishing how long even the responsible parts of society could turn a blind eye to it:

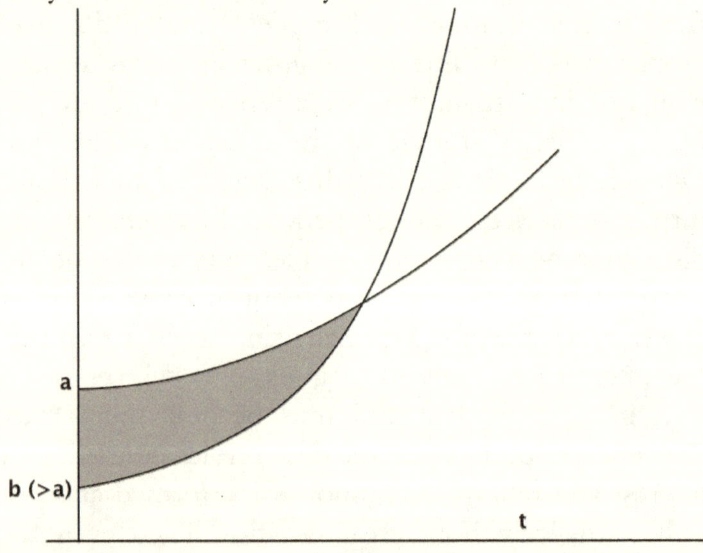

(The shaded part is the remaining purchasing power)

In this graph, "a" represents the curve of income (purchasing power of the individual or a household, tax revenue of a public purse or the national income or any other similar quantity), while "b" represents the curve of debt service including interest and compound interest or only interest and compound interest. According to this graph, the responsible creditor must avoid under all circumstances that—graphically speaking—the curve "b" rises steeper than the curve "a" and thus progressively reduces the remaining residual purchasing power towards zero.

This principle and the claim to the creditor that can be derived from it also applies to the case that occurs frequently enough, where a rise in the curve would occur despite the debt service that has been partially performed.

The verses following the quoted biblical passage, which deal with the taking of a pledge, probably show most clearly whether interest of any amount is justifiable:

> If thou at all take thy neighbor's raiment to pledge, thou shalt deliver it unto him by that the sun goeth down: For that is his covering only, it is his raiment for his skin: wherein shall he sleep?

With the question asked in the last line, the responsibility for the debtor's humane existence is clearly assigned to the creditor. Also the lending of money, the taking of interest and the seizure of pledged property is concerned with the relationship between humans, in which neither of the two sides may suffer serious damage in their human existence. Neither the anonymizing of money streams by the banks nor any contractual agreements or other social rules of the game can or must change anything about this. The lender of money assumes responsibility within the framework of the repayment and interest agreements for the debtor's humane existence or for ensuring that the debt service does not exceed the limit of humane existence. No more but also no less.

Here it becomes clear that interest as well as pledging must not lead to the existential endangerment of the debtor. This is a clear rejection, however, of any flat and uniformly constant interest rate, whether high or low. In this sense, interest is likely to skim off a share of prosperity, even if the interest taker almost always becomes an accomplice to injustice. He may never endanger the existence of the debtor.

This would require a variable interest rate not oriented on the problem of global money supply and economic management, as is common today, but oriented on the debtor's quite variable financial situation. With it we would pursue a direction that once was described to me by a banker from Sudan. He works mainly with (oil) money from the Saudis and where, because of the clear statements in the Koran, interest is forbidden but profit sharing is allowed.

Crucially important is that the interest does not remain a fixed value but at best represents a profit-sharing—if the term "interest" can then still be used at all. This is so important because interest in its current form is practically always included in cost accounting and calculation and is paid by the customer via the price. This applies to the goods and services of the economy as well as to public institutions, from cars to housing costs, electricity, sewage and hospitalization. The interest share of the directly or indirectly paid prices and costs of all goods and services ranges from 10 % for highly labor-intensive to 90 % for highly capital-intensive goods and services. Based on an average shopping cart of goods and services, the interest rate is around one third. So from every mark that the average citizen spends to earn a living, between 30 and 40 pfennigs are diverted to pay interest. The average citizen thus not only pays interest directly to his moneylenders, such as the bank, but also pays much more interest indirectly via the prices of the goods and services he buys.

The following breakdown of the population according to how affected they are by the interest system shows how bad this interest calculation actually looks:

Group 1:

All those people and ethnic groups who lose real purchasing power to an (often exponentially) growing extent due to our pricing and interest system, especially due to the compound interest effect, are the losers, up to and including the point of being bled dry and physical ruin.

Group 2:

All those who do not get into exponential progression on their debt but have a negative result in an interest rate differential calculation are the losers. This means that they pay more interest directly and indirectly than they earn. These are all those whose interest-bearing (or similarly increasing) assets are below—roughly speaking—a quarter of a million marks.

Group 3:

Winners in the interest calculation are all those whose interest income (or comparable forms of asset growth) is greater than the sum of their interest payments but for whom this positive difference is not so great as to lead to exponential development. As a rule, it serves luxury consumption from the more comfortable car to the beautiful apartment and on to the long vacation trip. Their money multiplication capacity lies —again roughly speaking—between a quarter of a million and a million marks.

Group 4:

The big parasites in the calculation of interest are all those whose monetary income is not used up in full but is at least partially re-invested and thus triggers the exponential development of the compound interest effect, whereby their financial assets increase explosively. Their multipliable financial assets are above one million marks. The vernacular rightly says that the first million costs work, afterwards anyone who continues to work hard is a jackass.

In German law, the above biblical claim is satisfied by the determination of the seizure limits in the individual law of obligations. As is well known, the debtor may not be seized in Germany below certain existential limits. Such a regulation does not exist in German corporate law nor in international law. A German company can go bankrupt and be dissolved, just as a debtor country can have the blood squeezed out of it by the International Monetary Fund. It is an open question as to where the boundaries should be drawn. In any case, it is a question that needs to be asked and discussed and which, at least in the international debt crisis, urgently requires a solution in the biblical sense. After all, the bare existence of millions of people is literally at stake.

What can we do?

It is a kind of double strategy. On the one hand, the consequences of the way we deal with money must be disclosed again and again. On the other hand, it is about acting responsibly and developing and promoting alternatives. With the Ecumenical Development Cooperative (EDCS) an important and right start has been made. However, this beginning should be expanded even more than before and supplemented by two decisive measures at the principle level.

The activities of the EDCS suffer mostly from the gambling house character of currency relations and price formation on the commodity markets. The borrower has no influence whatsoever on the exchange rate of the dollar or the D-Mark, currencies which usually provide the basis for the loan agreement. In the same way, he can hardly influence the final price of the products he produces over the term of the loan agreement. What, for example, coffee will cost in five years is written in the stars. The credit and commodity business is thus, on the one hand, a relationship on a serious economic basis, but on the other hand, to the same or even greater extent, pure speculation in the nature of what can be observed in gambling houses. This entails risks that ultimately cannot be expected of the borrower.

This difficulty can only be overcome if we develop the courage to have our own quasi-currency, which could be determined from the value of a shopping cart on the basis of reasonable prices at about the time of the credit negotiations, or even if repayment would be agreed in a clearly limited amount of natural produce (e.g. agricultural products), the distribution of which would be taken over by the trading networks of the so-called third or better one-world stores[58].

One last thing:

One of the fruits of our dealing with the problem of over-indebtedness is the so-called secondary market for debt securities of debtor countries. On this market, such securities are traded with value-adjusting discounts. It has become publicly known that Bolivian debt securities have been sold at discounts as low as 11% of their original value. This practice has positive and negative consequences, as the two examples below illustrate.

As we know, the World Wildlife Fund has purchased Bolivian debt securities with a nominal value of $1

58 Often now referred as "Fair Trade Stores" as is the one instigated by Haller in Trossingen, Germany.

million for $110,000 and transferred them to the government of Bolivia under an agreement under which a certain area of Bolivia is designated as a nature reserve and is exempt from technical development. Such a measure relieves the debtor country without encouraging inflation or other harmful developments.

The situation is different with steps that are basically similar to those that have become known from Volkswagen, for example. According to the information, Volkswagen has bought government bonds in Mexico at discounted prices and financed any investments there with the equivalent value in local currency, a measure that is clearly inflationary, not to mention that it means selling out to foreigners.

We know that the churches in their various bodies and at various levels have invested outrageous billions in interest-bearing assets[59]. It would be time to use increasing parts of these assets, for example within the framework of an ecumenical debt equalization fund, as a corrective to the murderous commodity and money economy of our time and thus to do justice to Jesus' statement that the members of God's people are the light of the world.

59 The EKD alone, i.e. the Protestant Church of Germany, had already raised over 700 million DM in interest in 1984. The billion mark has certainly long since been exceeded. This means that the financial assets invested (outside of old-age and risk provisions) are estimated to be between 15 and 20 billion DM and are of course also growing exponentially at the expense of the debtors, i.e. doubling in a cycle of 5 to 10 years (depending on the level of interest).

Labor and Income

Right to (gainful) employment

Among the basic social demands that were hotly debated in the last months of the former GDR, the right to work was one of the most important. As is well known, this question was raised again and again in our country but was always dismissed by the governing parties. Even the SPD and the large trade unions consider this right neither enforceable nor practicable. In any case, it does not seem worth the effort to fight for it. This is all the more astonishing, since unemployment is not really economically justifiable, let alone a human concern. For if an employee in an industrialized nation like the Federal Republic of Germany generates an average annual added value of at least 50,000 marks and thus not only generates purchasing power for himself personally but also a large sum of taxes and contributions. Then it becomes clear that every mass unemployment, as it has been observed almost everywhere for years, tears huge billion-dollar holes into every economic calculation.

Beyond that the experience (e.g. with us in the *Lebenshaus*) shows that the absence of a firm employment for (gainful) work, which also gives order and structure to the temporal process, endangers or even destroys the self-esteem and inner order of most humans. The same observation probably also applies to unpaid work, such as that performed by many housewives, whereby the purpose and structuring effect of this work seems to be based primarily on the fact that it extends beyond the fulfilment of one's individual needs.

It is quite conceivable that an industrial society such as ours would commit itself to offering a job to every person willing to work and, if necessary, to raise the required funds to finance it. This idea is not as far-fetched as it first appears. Rather, it has a centuries-old equivalent in Germanic land law. I know this from my own childhood experience. Until a few decades ago, for example, in the settlement areas of the Alemannic and Swabian peoples, it was possible and customary for every adult citizen to claim from his community for life the right to use a piece of land. This was referred to as the *Allmende* (commons), a piece of land that was ideally large enough to secure the minimum subsistence level for him and his family if it was properly worked.

The concept of social security with our ancestors did not aim at an unproductive basic income but rather at a safeguarding of the fundamentals for one's own earning of a minimum subsistence level. The *Allmende* and the restrictions connected with it and their advantages and disadvantages will not be discussed further here. The statement should suffice that the right to gainful employment today corresponds to the old right to common land.

In this context, it does not seem sensible or even superfluous to build up public companies and institutions for the employment of the otherwise unemployed via a state-financed second labor market. Rather, it should suffice to set up jobs everywhere in the same way as the job creation measures that have been common up to now—albeit to a very limited extent—in order to have a sufficient number of jobs available in the ups and downs of the economic cycle. This would help to avoid any unemployment that goes beyond personal transition issues. The unemployed should be granted the highest possible degree of co-determination in the selection of suitable jobs. Ideally, co-determination could be extended to the applicant's own search and selection within the framework set by the approval procedure.

This new type of job creation scheme should therefore act as a kind of employment buffer for the ups and downs of an economy. This variability would be feasible if the subsidies were approved for a limited period of time, for a period of at least one year. The number of job subsidies to be approved each year would also depend on the local or regional labor market situation.

In order to prevent the risk of subsidizing cheap labor for the economy, this job creation market should be strictly limited to the non-profit sector. This restriction would probably have to be extended to include large families, i.e. either families with a large number of children or with certain care tasks, especially care tasks for the elderly, for example. The job creation market would thus primarily comprise non-profit associations, which might even be founded primarily for this purpose. In addition there would be institutions of the free welfare service. In the latter case, it would have to be ensured that job creation positions could only be filled once the available budget had been fully utilized. In this way, it could be avoided that job creation schemes are misused as a stopgap and competitor for full-time workers, as seems to be the case with some people doing community service today.

As has been the case in the past, the job creation market should be administered and financed by the labor administration, i.e. the employment offices. The funds for this would have to come from unemployment insurance and should in individual cases account for 50 to 100% of the personnel costs incurred. The yardstick for the level of income would be the applicable tariffs for the work in question.

The percentage of the subsidy could be made dependent on the extent to which the person in question can be placed and used. Ultimately, it would even depend on the labor market situation, especially if—as seems necessary—each employment office were required to provide and offer an adequate number of places for all unemployed persons.

Reform of unemployment insurance

With a right to gainful employment to be secured in this way, it would be appropriate to reform the system of unemployment insurance, both in terms of the way it is financed and the length of time it is taken up.

As is well known, unemployment insurance today in Germany is funded in equal parts by employers and employees from the wage bill. Calculatively, these contributions increase personnel costs. They therefore put humans at a competitive disadvantage compared to machines, put labor-intensive companies at a disadvantage and give preference to capital-intensive ones. This injustice could be eliminated by the fact that although the employee's share is still deducted from the gross wage as a solidarity contribution and therefore remains part of the personnel costs, the employer's share will in future be calculated from the total value added including exports. In other words, the total corporate income consisting of personnel costs, interest and profit (before taxes). It is particularly important to include the cost of capital—above all interest—in this calculation. This means that social costs must also be included. According to the generally accepted idea, the cost of capital corresponds to the personnel costs. They should therefore not be excluded from such a burden. Yes, it would even have to be considered whether they could be increased by the depreciation, since a reduction of the "labour market value" of the employee is not considered for tax purposes either.

Admittedly, from the human point of view it is really a frightening idea to compare man with the machine. However, in the present case this seems to be quite appropriate for the sake of justice for man. This is all the more so as the usual business management approach does not deal with the matter in a different manner.

As far as the duration of unemployment insurance is concerned, it would be conceivable to make it even more dependent on the duration of employment and the payment of contributions. If for each year of contribution payment an entitlement to insurance benefits of one month's duration were to be granted, this would primarily benefit older workers, who are usually the main victims of the trend. After thirty years of employment, for example, entitlement to unemployment insurance would be guaranteed for a period of thirty months.

The second stage, namely unemployment assistance, could possibly be completely omitted, since a sufficient number of jobs would be available for all those willing to work. As far as this would release funds in an economy-wide calculation (taking into account the longer insurance entitlement for older employees), these could be used to finance the job creation schemes.

After unemployment insurance there would be possibly thus only the direct step to welfare assistance.

Such a reduction of unemployment benefits would of course put enormous pressure on the unemployed to take up one of the offered jobs after the expiration of the unemployment insurance. Therefore it would have to be particularly carefully regulated. It would have to be decided which jobs are reasonable according to their burden and requirement, according to their distance from the place of residence and according to their payment, taking into consideration the human dignity of the persons concerned.

Welfare or minimum income?

Whether however social welfare assistance should be extended according to the repeated demand for the granting of a minimum income, is a completely different question. There are many things to consider.

On the one hand, a person runs the risk of becoming psychologically debilitated if his livelihood is publicly assured. The exercise of an appropriate gainful employment seems to be a blessing rather than a curse. In any case, it not only gives human life meaning and purpose, it also gives it a temporal rhythm and framework that is extremely helpful for most people. Experience seems to show that the dangers for humans are greater when there is a lack of work than vice versa. Perhaps this only applies to countries such as the Federal Republic of Germany, where people are hardly capable of constant leisure, which is why we attach great importance to gainful employment.

On the other hand, a system of this kind promotes a sense of entitlement that is independent of the willingness to perform, as we can observe with the various forms of insurance, where almost everyone tries to get the most out of as little effort as possible. Beyond that, nothing is done to promote solidarity and responsibility in thinking and acting among the others. On the contrary. They only see the apparently well-fed idler, who becomes a parasite and has to be fed by them.

As is well known, solidarity and responsibility and ultimately community can only grow in a manageable space. These are areas of a magnitude in which people are not just numbers or figures to each other but have faces, names and destinies. For the sake of this solidarity and responsibility and for the sake of the fact that both are indispensable for every community, it must become a main concern of every social policy to promote the emergence of such spaces. With regard to our concern, this means that jobs must be created and financed in decentralized and citizen-managed areas. It is quite conceivable that employment, especially of less stable people, could be promoted, supported and, if necessary, monitored by professional helpers employed by the employment offices, the municipalities or the districts. However, the providers and thus the guarantors of full employment should always be decentralized groupings. In this way, they should also become learning and training grounds for solidarity and responsibility, if possible for everyone. After all, in a democracy it cannot only be a matter of citizens interfering in politics as demanding and criticizing parties. They must also learn to think and act increasingly in a self responsible manner.

There is a considerable discrepancy between the socially important right to a state guarantee of a minimum income for everyone and the reality in which the unemployed become, are and will remain socially isolated. Many of them therefore suffer damage in their humanity in the long run. This plight is not remedied even by more money, because it is mainly due to our behavior and the size of social groups and spaces. With further development of the above described insight about the importance of "manageable space", it becomes clear that the willingness of humans to provide for their livelihood is inversely proportional to the internal and/or external distance, if necessary even without appropriate "compensation". Thereby the willingness to show solidarity and the demand for performance complement each other one hundred percent, as the following diagram shows:

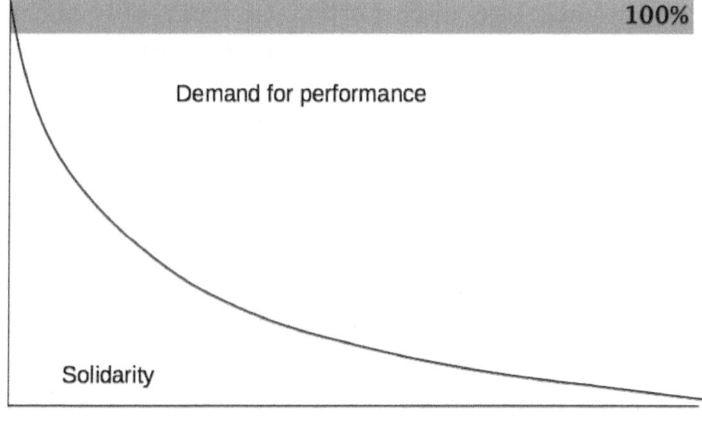

The first section (at the left margin of the graph), is the core community. It is quite conceivable (in fact also common, e.g. in marriage towards the non-working partner and young children, in some countries also towards parents and forefathers) to distribute or grant income and/or to finance the subsistence through solidaristic thinking and acting independently of any "consideration" to be provided or expected from the beneficiary. Here and only in this circle the idea of a complete separation of work and income has its place. It may be left open how great the inner and outer distance can be in order to be able to remain with a solidarity willingness of 100% and a performance requirement of 0%. It is important to note that this limit must not be exceeded in order to avoid bad blood among those who are forced to show solidarity and to avoid a sense of entitlement among the beneficiaries.

As the distance increases, we move on to the next section, in which the mean value of solidarity and performance requirements are balanced. In other words, performance is required on the one hand, but solidarity is also practiced on the other. The solidarity thought stands in the foreground, if for instance the income level is determined primarily by needs and not by achievement. In contrast to such a permanent solution, in our large society solidarity is usually only granted in a limited form for exceptional situations, such as continued payment of wages in case of illness. Here, in the event of occupational disability due to illness, there is usually a switch from benefit entitlement to solidarity for a period of six weeks, that is, for a limited period.

In the rightmost section, i.e. at the greatest inner and/or outer distance, (almost) only the performance requirement prevails. It therefore applies above all to trade relations with suppliers and freelancers. Usually fixed prices and other conditions are negotiated and contractually agreed upon. Any difficulties that arise for the party obliged to perform are of little interest. Whether or not the partner can live in an appropriate manner under the agreed conditions is also of little interest. Since these conditions are subject to the laws of the market, from exchange rate fluctuations to price erosion in the event of oversupply or shrinking demand, it is not uncommon for bad business relationships to arise. The weaker party is ruthlessly exploited and plundered, as many employment relationships and business relations on a small and large scale make clear. Let us only think of the so-called Third World in this respect.

In the story of the vineyard workers from the Greek Bible[60], Jesus tells of a householder who at various times "hired" day laborers[61] to work in his vineyard and paid them all the same wage in the evening, even though some had a full day's work, while those who were hired last had only a short time to work. This is a typical example of a need wage instead of a performance wage.

With this story, Jesus provides a model for a far-reaching solidarity with the hired day laborers (but only with these), in which the otherwise usual demand for performance is only related to the more or less long working hours. The paid standard wage was without a doubt a daily wage and thus high enough to enable the necessary purchases to earn a living at least for the next day.

It is essential—and this seems to be a problem of intellectual horizons, consciousness and ultimately ethics —to extend the second circle ever further. This is necessary in order to give increasing space to the idea of solidarity with others, despite all the justification of the demand for performance. What in military thinking represents the idea of a security partnership, in

60 Matt. 20.

61 Note, as the term already makes clear, that on this path man threatens to become a thing, an object, a tool.

economic relations would be the consideration of the vital interests of the respective partner. In the end, the inner and/or outer distance should lose importance. This corresponds to the introduction of the concept of the neighbor in Judeo-Christian thinking that can be seen in the quoted story of Jesus.

An old Jewish illustration makes the necessary development particularly clear:

A student asked the Rabbi, "How should one determine when night has ended and day begun?" "It is when you look into the face of a stranger and see your sister or brother," said the Rabbi.[62]

That is the point.

The structure described makes it clear how solidarity and the demand for performance have become reality in the economic and social structures in which each and every one of us is integrated. In the large churches we find the innermost circle once again with the alimentation principle for the pastors—but only for

62 https://www.templeisraelcenter.org/wp-content/uploads/2020/01/Parashat-Vayishlach_RA-1.pdf. Interpreted by Rabbi Annie Tucker: "I believe there is another, deeper, level of meaning to the Hasidic story, however, a meditation on bringing peace and healing that is found in the rabbi's poignant response to his students. "It is when you look into the face of a stranger and see your sister or brother," said the rabbi. "Until then, night is still with us." It is only when we look at someone we do not know and see them as a fellow child of God, a person worthy of inherent dignity and respect, that we can overcome the darkness that so often plagues modern society. Until we feel a sense of responsibility for the stranger, a sense of connection to the other, night – indeed – is still very much upon us."

them—with the idea of the solidarity-based granting of income without a compulsory demand for performance. But since the "circle of solidarity" is too large, i.e. solidarity no longer comes from a community but from an institution, the original approach is lost. This leads to the social learning of solidarity for both the givers and the takers. In the Free Churches, which pay their pastors from the local community, i.e. rather from active communities, we can usually observe the second phase of our structure today. However, classical employer thinking is often applied here to determine income. This means that the granting of income is not only linked to a compulsion to perform but also to a detailed right of the paying persons to give directives. Often enough, it is not even felt that in a community of solidarity, everyone is obliged to take over and fulfill certain tasks within the appropriate organs, according to their own possibilities and limitations and on their own volition. In the end, they do this completely independently of whether they receive more or less large financial contributions from the solidarity community to secure their livelihood[63]. The fact that the person "made available" and financially secured for such tasks takes over more of these tasks than the person who is professionally engaged elsewhere, is actually all the more self-evident as this person "made available" has mostly decided for these tasks himself. However, this has nothing to do with the payer's direct right to issue directives because of having made the payment.

63 See also "Right to issue directives and self-determination".

These structures can hardly be influenced or even changed by most of us. Since the implementation of such changes in political work takes a lot of time, it becomes indispensable to create own structures together with like-minded people in order to realize the necessary changes and also to practice this solidarity in the sense of social learning. The ideal framework for this is the creation of a solidarity fund, usually within the framework of a non-profit association, through which friends are "made available" to work on certain tasks that are important to the community and that cannot be done voluntarily on their own. The financial needs for their livelihood would be fully or partially borne by the community, i.e. financed from the solidarity fund.

The Right to Issue Directives and Self-Determination

Hardly anywhere else is the discrepancy between aspirations and reality, between ethical theory and everyday practice, as clear as in the organizational structures of our working world. Here, omnipotence and the obsession with indispensability celebrate triumphs every day and the subject is considered an indispensable organism. If the usual way of thinking and behaving is to be questioned, this must be done above all in our working world. This is all the more so because most people spend a large part of their day in it and their personal human development depends very much on it.

When it comes to the question of optimum administrative and management structures in the diverse places of work, it is important to make a strict distinction between the areas of administration and management. Only objects and things can be administered but not people, even if we not only keep on pretending to do so, as the name of many positions makes clear, but also endeavor to do so.

The question of authorization rights is contentious and requires appropriate regulation in the area of administration. Are they to be centralized or decentralized, or are we dealing with mixed forms of central and decentralized authority? If authorization rights are tied to several places or persons, the rules of the game are important, according to which decisions are made —by consensus or by majority. It is possible that there will still the lonely decision "by virtue of office", i.e. due to a higher hierarchical position. In these border-line cases both concern and expertise are overridden as factors of entitlement to participate in the decision-making process.

According to the law relating to associations, for example, decision-making rights are established and legitimized "by virtue of office" through the election of an executive committee. They can be defused however with good will completely simply by the fact that, for example, executive committee meetings are open in principle for all club members and a right of codetermination and participation is granted to these also. So that such meetings are not only de jure but also de facto generally accessible, it may however be necessary to set them on a usually fixed date. For instance, this could be every first Monday evening of the month/quarter, so that it does not happen that nobody apart from the board of directors knows in time due to appointments and corresponding information or lack of information. In any case, the decision-making rights in the internal relationship do not necessarily have to be congruent with those legally prescribed for the external relationship. This means that the board of directors, which is required by law and is indispensable for clear relations with the outside world, does not need to have the sole right to make decisions internally. However, involving others in the decision-making process requires clear rules, for example, taking into account the principles of concern and expertise. Moreover, openness and transparency are indispensable basic concerns.

Often in everyday life such rather tricky questions that expose what people really think and the way they behave. They are quite simply circumvented by the fact that everybody has different rights of decision making. Thus, a clear, albeit depressing, decision is made on the question of power. After all, the availability or non-availability of money ultimately determines not only how we deal with objects or things but also how we employ and pay people. Money becomes the decisive power factor.

However, these are all problems of secondary importance. Of course, the consideration of human dignity and the image of God has to do with the right of disposal, especially of money, as the following example shows:

The position of secretary of a parish office of the Archdiocese of Freiburg had been cut back more and more in the course of church austerity measures. First from a full-time position to a part-time position and finally to a weekly hourly workload that was below the social security limits, thus enabling the employer to make further savings. The pastor in charge fought this development to the best of his ability. He would also have been willing to cede a portion of his income (on the gross wage rate of course) in favor of his secretary, in order to spare her the existentially problematic reduction in income. All efforts remained without success.

This story makes two things clear:

On the one hand it is a legitimate right of the church management to decide on savings corresponding to its income development, that is, the amount of church tax revenues. Such decisions must also be passed on to the bodies affected by them. However, here the management's authority to make decisions also has to stop. Even if the aggregation of all sources of income in the large churches is not questioned at a central point, i.e. at the level of the dioceses or regional churches, the general distribution practice must still be criticized. That is the second point.

This distribution practice cannot be matched with a positive image of man, the image of God as a human being. In addition, the church employee "officially" does not get the opportunity to professionally practice one of the central Christian concerns, namely sharing or solidarity.

This would be quite easy to achieve with a regulation that decides on the staffing plans and income structures in accordance with the collective agreements or agreements similar to collective agreements. However, this would only result in aggregated totals for certain function groups, e.g. a city municipality or a dean's office. However, the distribution of these totals should be left to the function groups that would be granted autonomy of distribution in this way. To ensure that such a distribution does not result in anything being fixed in the long term and with consequential burdens for job successors, it would have to suffice to limit the duration of deviations. This would have to be done in accordance with the staffing plans and the classification associated with them. It would require constant renegotiation and agreement.

The question is where sharing and solidarity should really be exercised and practiced, if not in the employment relationship and in the income from work. This can be seen in the next example (after all, it is time that something positive also be discussed):

In a post-operative hospital in the Swabian region of Germany, two and a half physician positions were planned. When half of the vacant position was to be filled by a family man who would not have been able to meet his financial obligations with half an income, the other doctors decided, with the consent of their sponsor, to put all two and a half positions into one pot and divide them by three. With more than 80% of a normal income, all three of them and their families make a pretty good financial living. So there are other ways of doing things. In most cases, however, it is not so much the willingness of those involved that is lacking but rather the structure and above all the stubbornness of the employer. And that is a pity.

In addition to exposing the problems associated with the rights of decision-making, especially over money, it is important to realize that man cannot and must not be administered if he is not to be a subject, degraded to an object and deprived of the dignity of his godly likeness.

This demand seems at first to be nothing more than a noble ethical claim that everyday reality in our organizations, including those of the church, is not able to meet. And yet, the Christian social ethics which has pursued these questions and come to rather radical conclusions has become a much more visible and tangible reality in modern management doctrine and in its implementation in progressive business enterprises than is known to the vast majority of churchmen. In fact, most church offices and other institutions lag far behind the current state of development of management theory and practice in their organizational structures. This is highly regrettable because Christian social ethics has done important theoretical groundwork for the development of management theory, even though this is rarely acknowledged. One reason for this may be that the representatives of modern management rarely admit to any religious or even church ties. On the other hand, the discrepancy between claim and reality, specifically between social ethics and organizational reality in the church, is mostly "a disgrace for the guild". Thus, even from well-meaning quarters, the described connection between Christian social ethics and modern management is ashamedly not demonstrated publicly.

To avoid giving the impression of polemics, it is necessary to describe claim and possibility in this fashion.

In the magnificent publication "Vision" by CARITAS, "Principles, goals and strategies for inpatient care for the elderly in the 1990s", the terms "Personality, subsidiarity, solidarity and universality" are described as the basic concepts of Catholic social teaching. Under "subsidiarity" the following can be read:

"The basic principle of subsidiarity.... results from the personality of the human being.

In the organization of every human community, the individual and the respective smaller groups have the right and the duty to arrange their affairs themselves, as far as they are able to do so. If they are not able to do so, viable partners provide help for self-help. Even necessary long-term help is help for self-help because every human being lives his or her own life".

What does this mean in organizational practice, and what does modern management theory say about it?

The most important and radical consequence of this is the renunciation of the right of command.

Such a sentence will initially make every conservative organizational specialist's hair stand on end. And yet this principle works. Of course, it is not about giving everyone the right to change and operate as they please without having to consider instructions "from above". That would open the door to chaos. Rather, the principles of "Management by Objectives" (MBO)[64], i.e. management by agreement on objectives,

64 Management by objectives (MBO), also known as management by results (MBR), was first popularized by Peter Drucker in his 1954 book The Practice of Management. Management by objectives is the process of defining specific objectives within an organization that management can convey to organization members, then deciding how to achieve each objective in sequence. This process allows managers to take work that needs to be done one step at a time to allow for a calm, yet productive work environment. This process also helps organization members to see their accomplishments as they achieve each objective, which reinforces a positive work environment and a sense of achievement. An important part of MBO is the measurement and comparison of an employee's actual performance with the standards set. Ideally, when employees themselves have been involved with the goal-setting and choosing the course of action to be followed

are applied in a similar way to the negotiation of contracts between equals. These negotiations to agree on objectives are conducted at regular intervals, firstly for a kind of agreement in principle before or when the applicant is hired and later normally at annual intervals. The agreement in principle is automatically and regularly updated.

The agreement in principle and its annual supplement usually replace the widely used job description. They differ from it mainly in that they are consciously considered and treated as dynamic and changeable and not as static, as is usually the case with job descriptions. After all, the latter are often elaborated once enough when the person is hired or even only when the position is established. They then slumber away for years, so that they finally become museum pieces that correspond to a time long past.

Since the negotiations on the agreement in principle only lead to an agreement if the tasks are to be fulfilled in such a way as seems to be correct in the con-

by them, they are more likely to fulfill their responsibilities. According to George S. Odiorne, the system of management by objectives can be described as a process whereby the superior and subordinate jointly identify common goals, define each individual's major areas of responsibility in terms of the results expected of him or her, and use these measures as guides for operating the unit and assessing the contribution of each of its members. MBO refers to the process of setting goals for the employees so that they know what they are supposed to do at the workplace. Management by Objectives defines roles and responsibilities for the employees and help them chalk out their future course of action in the organization. (Wikipedia).

text of the entire organization according to the interpretation of the recruiters. Naturally, only those applicants are recruited whose own ideas do not conflict with the overall objectives. Wild growth is therefore impossible despite the renunciation of authority to issue directives. This also applies to the annual supplementary agreements, so that the concerns of conservative professionals are actually unfounded.

The adherence to or fulfillment of the target agreements is jointly reviewed on a regular basis. This makes it clear how important it is to have transparency in the description of tasks and the timing of goal setting. It must be clear how the person concerned has to fulfill his or her tasks with what support from which persons and with what aids and above all at what times.

Manageable and realizable scope and time are important. Most people are not able to organize and manage complex tasks over long periods of time and to have the stamina to cope with the resulting tension. This must be taken into account. The easiest way to achieve this is to divide large tasks into subtasks or sections and to agree on the appropriate times. For example, it is easier to meet the agreed targets for a comprehensive report if a time for completion is set for each section or chapter of the report. This breakdown not only provides multiple control points for internal and external control. It also provides the occasions for a sense of achievement, which are extremely important for motivation.

If discrepancies between agreement and reality become apparent during the joint review of the goal setting agreements, or if difficulties arise in the cooperation between several employees that they are not able to resolve themselves, then the supervisor can take action. Under the term "Management by Exception" (MBE) he has the right to intervene in exceptional cases, i.e. to suspend the self-determination rights of the respective employees—but only in exceptional cases.

MBO and MBE drastically change the classic role of the supervisor. The leadership role is actually shifting from a ruling to a serving one. It is primarily aimed at coordinating the functions of those to be led towards common goals and ensuring that this is the case when agreeing on goals and fulfilling them. Thus, the task of the superior is primarily aimed at helping the others to fulfill their tasks.

A simple example shows that the path described is quite reasonable and feasible:

If someone decides to work as a driver in a company, the contract naturally includes who tells him under what conditions and requirements the tasks he has to perform as a driver. That this information does not represent a right to give instructions in the actual sense is shown by the simple fact that it can certainly come from a "hierarchical" and lower-income colleague, such as a scheduler, and not from a classic boss with the right to give instructions. In this concrete example, the decisive factor would be the decision on the route, where the driver is without doubt the more competent person. Due to his daily experience, he is better able to avoid, for example, construction sites and rush hour traffic in time bottlenecks than would be the case with a route specification stubbornly conceived at a desk according to the map.

In this way, the legacy of Jesus becomes an organizational possibility. As we all know, according to the traditions, he said on the last supper, "With you it must be different. The highest among you must be like the lowest and the leader like the subordinate". The MbE principle also takes into account the concern of the subsidiarity principle to transfer power and decision-making powers to higher hierarchical levels only when the respective lower level is overburdened for whatever reason.

The interventions "from above" that are possible through MBE also correspond to the rule described by Martin Buber for structures largely free of domination, according to which coercive measures are (only) necessary and permissible at all levels of society up to the limits of personal responsibility. However, the decisive factor here is whether the disputed grey area between personal and external responsibility or self-determination and determination by others out of a rather dirigiste or patriarchal pessimism ("things do go wrong after all") combined with a negative image of man ("man is evil from youth on") is claimed "from above". Or on the other hand, whether this grey area is conceded up to the critical limit as a field for learning and practice, even if something goes wrong from time to time. Thus simply offering the person an opportunity to grow and mature.

This can be represented graphically as follows:

In every community situation, from the family to the

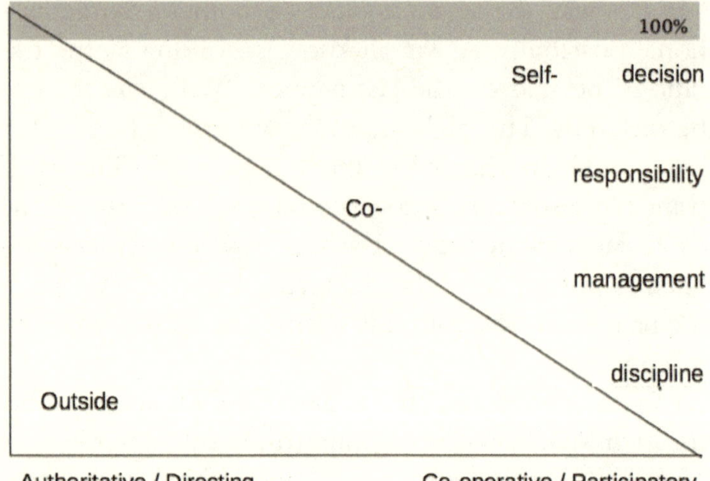

community, from the company to the large corporation, self-determination, responsibility and discipline—graphically represented—must complement each other to the sum of 100% through outside determination, responsibility and discipline in order to regulate a generally beneficial community life. The more the structure is authoritarian/directing, the more the emphasis is on "**outside...**", i.e. most of the things are "imposed from above". The more the structure is cooperative/participatory, the more the emphasis must shift towards self-control ("self-..."). This is clearly visible in the diagram. At the vertical line at the extreme left edge the foreign control prevails, while at the vertical line at the extreme right edge self control prevails. In between, there are various gradations or combinations between the two extremes, as the vertical line, drawn at any point in our graphic, illustrates.

Basically it can be said that the former corresponds more to the Caesars, i.e. is Roman imperialist and leads to a kind of PAX ROMANA, while the latter corresponds more to the Messiah and aims at the PAX CHRISTI. It is clear to every practitioner that there are always mixed forms between the two in a "Kingdom of God" that has only just begun. Therefore, MBO is also supplemented by MBE. However, it is decisive whether the organizational structures keep the path, i.e. organizational development, to cooperation and participation, i.e. in the diagram to the right, open and open again and again, or whether the opposite is the case. In the one case it is a matter of a growing measure of freedom, in the other of coercion imposed "from above". that the growing measure of freedom must be supplemented by an equal measure of responsibility, goes without saying, since freedom and responsibility are the two different sides of the same coin.

Working according to the principles of MBO and MBE makes it possible to meet high ethical standards in organizations of all kinds, not only in theory and according to the good will of individuals, but also in daily practice, even in their structures.

The fact that the term organizational development (American "Organizational Development or OD)[65] is

65 Organization development (OD) is the study of successful organizational change and performance. OD emerged from human relations studies in the 1930s, during which psychologists realized that organizational structures and processes influence worker behavior and motivation. More recently, work

mentioned here shows a further insight of modern management theory. It takes into account the fact that organizational changes usually not only require or result in changes in behavior but also in consciousness. And, as is well known, this takes time. Therefore, we are not talking about dramatic, revolutionary upheavals but about the readiness for continuous change. However, this insight should not be misused to work in good old church tradition using the yardstick of centuries. Time has already run out for us anyway. And Jesus did not say, "You are the *back* light of the world."

One of the most massive bulwarks that should collapse in the course of this continuous change is the right to unilaterally assess "subordinate" employees for entry into their personnel files. This evaluation is usually carried out once a year and then disclosed in an appraisal interview between superior and subordinate. It is not rarely disputed as to how far the disclosure goes. For instance, whether or not the employee can inspect his or her personnel file at any time.

An evaluation system that would correspond to our ethical insights would include a mutual evaluation be-

on OD has expanded to focus on aligning organizations with their rapidly changing and complex environments through organizational learning, knowledge management and transformation of organizational norms and values. Key concepts of OD theory include: organizational climate (the mood or unique "personality" of an organization, which includes attitudes and beliefs that influence members' collective behavior), organizational culture (the deeply-seated norms, values and behaviors that members share) and organizational strategies (how an organization identifies problems, plans action, negotiates change and evaluates progress). (Wikipedia).

tween all those who regularly work together. As a result, they not only get to know each other, but are also dependent on each other in the fulfilment of their tasks. This type of evaluation should be less an assessment because it easily leads to condemnation but rather a subjective determination of how different personal characteristics and functions are perceived by oneself and others. In this process, self-perception and the perception of others must be compared in a dialog in order to reveal weaknesses, misunderstandings and misjudgements and thus be able to correct them.

I recall an incident where in one such process, when an employee was asked about his listening skills, he gave himself a high score, meaning that he was a good listener, while all his communication partners gave him a low score. The obvious discrepancy between self-perception and the perception of others was used as an opportunity for a clarifying conversation, which proved to be extremely helpful and liberating for all involved.

All this makes it clear that the one-sided emphasis on the question of task fulfillment alone is not sufficient to develop healthy living organizational structures. Modern management theory states that in addition to "locomotion", i.e. the promotion of goal-oriented task fulfillment, equal attention must be paid to "cohesion", i.e. the internal cohesion of employees. A closer look reveals that the terms "locomotion" and "cohesion" originate from an old Christian tradition. They correspond not only to the collective but also to the individual internal or external environment and are thus also related to the terms “praying and working” or “faith and works”.

In concrete terms, this means that not only technical and professional training and further education must be promoted but also the ability to work together and to resolve conflicts in a friendly and warm-hearted manner. As general experience shows, it is not uncommon for the simplest things to be lacking. If I just look at an elaborate conference for the solution of any task, it is already apparent from the often very unproductive process that most of the participants have no idea of an optimally executed decision-making process. It is not uncommon for one person to be talking about possible solutions while the other person hasn’t even grasped what it’s all about (he hasn’t read the presentation). The third is asleep, while the fourth sees his task primarily in defending his position, and the fifth is involved in a trench war against the sixth. No wonder that the harvest is meager after hours of debate.

Of course, general knowledge of normal conference techniques would not make better people out of the participants. However, it would show how amateurish and ridiculous many are, both in terms of locomotion and cohesion. This alone, as examples show, could have a very beneficial effect.

But acquiring the necessary knowledge and skills for such things is less a question of wanting or not wanting. It becomes more and more a question of having to.

Our organizational structures are changing from hierarchical fir tree structures with isolated lone fighters to living organisms with networked structures of more or less autonomous teams. Even the church and its various institutions cannot close themselves off from this development in the long run.

The Blindness of The German Protestant Church

In an almost spooky way, the Economic Memorandum of the Protestant Churches of Germany (EKD)[66], published in the fall of 1991, makes clear their intertwining and entanglement with the "Western" economic system. This entanglement does not rank behind the worse examples of the church's attitude to the social system, neither in the so-called Third Reich nor in the former GDR. This intertwining is not only to be found in the Protestant churches, however. In all of Germany's major churches, a great unanimity with the basic economic and political convictions of our country can be observed. This is not surprising, since these fundamental convictions are supported by all the major German parties in a kind of social consensus. The churches, too, make their contribution to this basic consensus, a contribution that is favorable to the majority.

In the analysis section the memorandum is gratifyingly sincere. This means that it is also critical, al-

66 Although this chapter is devoted to discussing the hypocrisy of a paper issued by the German Protestant Church, the reader will note that this is equally relevant for other nations and religious organizations.

though its criticism is not fundamental but at best cosmetic. It focuses on certain individual points, such as the employers' goal of switching more and more to working on Sundays, a goal against which the churches together with the trade unions are putting up great resistance. However, when it comes to not only asking questions after the analysis section but trying to find answers from the biblical tradition, the paper remains strangely void. And so, with this memorandum, the Protestant churches sing their part in the great jubilant chorus. This part could just as well have been composed by some liberal, non-church business experts. The theological statements seem rather artificial and remain foreign bodies. They are recognizably written by others than the authors of the economic section and have little or nothing to do with it. It is not possible to develop standards for evaluating the theory and practice of our economy from the Judeo-Christian traditions and theology and to derive conclusions in keeping with the times.

When taking stock, the memorandum hardly reaches the critical level of the Brandt Commission's North-South Report or the Carter Commission's "Global 2000" report. Groundbreaking impulses, as they would not only be expected from a Jesuanic interpretation of the biblical standards, but are even to be demanded by an increasingly helpless public, are almost completely missing. Thus the third section of the memorandum, which deals with "business as a place of Christian responsibility," is lost in aloof slogans. Their noncommittal nature can be recognized by the fact that, like similar proclamations of other churches, they can be parroted by anyone, whether honest man or swindler, without hesitation and without pangs of conscience. This begins with the question, "What does it mean to understand business as a place of Christian responsibility? (page 46[67]). This is followed on the same page by the lofty claim, "The church is guided by the biblical testimony of God's justice and the message of God's love....,"—a claim which on the whole proves to be an empty formula. If there were at least a modest admission that it is about trying to interpret this biblical witness. But we did not have to worry about that—in any case, the retraction comes immediately afterwards. "Questions of economic order should not be elevated to the rank of confessions. To make this sufficiently clear for everyone, it is later said, "However, the Bible is not a recipe book from which instructions for certain measures in business and politics can be taken directly." (page 49). As the report shows, it is not even about indirectly deriving instructions from the Bible. In any case, hardly anyone would have expected anything so direct.

Obviously, different standards are applied. So the question of the Sabbath rest takes (fortunately) a lot of space. As for the question of money, the biblical prohibition of interest is not even mentioned with a single word. That the Sabbath rest is to be found in the ten commandments, the prohibition of interest on the other hand is "only" a part of the Mosaic, i.e. divine instruction, cannot excuse this omission, the

67 Page numbers according to the EPD 42/91 documentation.

more so that our kind of money economy constantly demands great human sacrifices.

In order to avoid all possible disquiet, the non-binding nature of biblical ethics for our relationship with God is further emphasized, "The measure of our ethical responsibility is not the measure by which we are measured by God" (page 49). Even when taken in context, this remains an evil word, especially in an economic-ethical memorandum, since it ultimately means that the mistreatment and downfall of man and nature as a result of an economic mis-development actively shaped by man has little or nothing to do with our relationship with God.

Moreover, this statement is in direct contradiction to the demand for "stewardship in the living space of the earth" (page 50), of which it says among other things, "Man is called by his destiny to actively preserve and shape the earth. For the fulfillment of this task, as a creature among creatures, he is given by God the living space of the earth and the time of his life. This does not mean absolute dominion, but stewardship...". Does this mean ethical responsibility for the Christian standing before God and his criteria or not? Or does this only apply to nature and not also to our fellow men?

With the above quoted clean bill of health for all inhumanity as a theological basis, a paper was created that should provide a tranquil conscience and an undisturbed night's rest even for the worst of greed and economic inhumanity.

Admittedly, the memorandum begins quite sincerely in its analysis of our situation. It speaks of "problems of historical proportions, such as the threat to the natural foundations of life and the impoverishment of large parts of the world's population" (page 7). It goes on to say that "In one way or another, all damaging influences of humans on the biosphere are part or consequence of their economic actions" (page 8). Consequently, the question is then posed, "How must the economy be organized in order to achieve a social and life-sustaining optimization of the dimensions of livelihood security, social compatibility and environmental friendliness? (page 8). This question is still being asked and unfortunately remains ultimately unanswered therein.

The question of "social justice on an international scale" is raised with similar clarity. It speaks of a "dramatic challenge". Correctly it says, "The rich countries are getting richer and richer, the poor are getting poorer and poorer" (page 10). It also concedes, "Many developing countries... are particularly hard hit by the fall in prices when there is an oversupply of these raw materials". (page 10). The international debt crisis is also addressed. Of the highly indebted countries, it is said, "Quite a few of them now spend almost half of their current export earnings on interest and redemption payments." (page 10). However, the answer to the blatant problem remains more than meager. At the end of the few lines on the world debt crisis, the following is succinctly stated, "... the International Monetary Fund (IMF), in cooperation with the World Bank, is now working on a strategy of adjustment that is more in line with development." (page 11)

The fact that the IMF and the World Bank act as agents for the creditors—like a goat turned into a gardener—is discreetly concealed. That they never really solved the debt problems out of this role, as all the debt rescheduling agreements of the past show, but only gained time as a reprieve for their clients, the reader learns nothing about that, nor about the consequences of these debt rescheduling agreements. In general, the world debt problem, which kills thousands of people every day, is treated practically only in the manner of a subordinate clause. There is no critical word about our monetary system, although in the Bible, both in the so-called Old Testament and in Jesus[68], there is always talk of money and interest. In this document however, it is obvious that the Bible does not provide instructions for the economy.

The fact that interest has an offspring dangerous to the public—compound interest—which not only concerned the authors of the Bible but even the fathers of the German Civil Code, who wanted to see it treated differently from interest under the law of obligations—does not seem to affect the authors of the Protestant Church memorandum. However, compound interest, whenever it occurs, leads to an economically catastrophic, exponential, i.e. ultimately explosive, increase in financial assets on the one hand and in debts on the other. The consequences for the victims are murderous. This seems to be either completely unknown or not even worth mentioning.

68 e.g. "do good to them, and lend to them without expecting to get anything back" (Luke 6.35).

The analysis of the world situation is followed by an honest account of the national situation. There is talk of permanent unemployment as well as of the "new poverty". The fact that "the top earners accumulate about as much wealth as all statistically recorded 26 million normal households combined" (page 13), as well as the statement that "at present the labor income ratio is... has reached its lowest level in three decades". (In plain language this means that ever larger portions of the national income flow to the money owners). Why this is so and with mathematical regularity is so, is not said. It is merely stated, "It is therefore understandable that the question of justice of distribution is raised as a matter of urgency" (page 14). Significantly, however, this question is not posed by the authors of the memorandum themselves, let alone affirmed or even answered. It is only legitimized as "understandable".

The blindness regarding the causes of our crises reaches its completion in the question of property. It begins with the half-truth, "Private ownership of the means of production enables the separation of powers between the state and the economy.... Where the state not only creates the legal framework for the economy but also owns the enterprises. Its claim to power cannot be challenged." (page 22) Starting from the negative examples in Eastern Europe, the authors pretend that there is no middle ground between state and private ownership. Private property is seen as the only sensible alternative to state ownership.

First of all, against this background, the social responsibility of property is recalled (Article 14.2 of the

Basic Law). Although this has in fact not been talked about for a long time. At least not as long as speculative residential property can be made uninhabitable without objection, so as not to have to make it accessible to unwanted tenants. Nor as long as in the economy the protection of company value and thus of property is more important than the jobs of employees (there are more than enough examples of both). None of this is mentioned. It remains lip service that does not pillory the constant abuse of property rights at the expense of social duty. On the contrary, private property is also being talked about as a decisive motivating factor in the economy:

"The abolition or denial of private property as an independent economic potential does not eliminate the dangers of abuse of public property....". Has anyone seriously claimed this? "It does, however, eliminate the awareness of the concrete obligation associated with property. It is, nonetheless, unmistakable that private property in the market economy performs an important and irreplaceable function for responsible economic activity." (p. 57) thus also "irreplaceable", to rule out any critical discussion from the outset, as if companies like Bosch or Mahle, to name just two, which as foundations are neither state nor private property, did not perform important functions in our economy.

Yet the Bible would provide a starting point for alternative thinking, since it always speaks of rights of use and not of private property in our, namely pre-Christian-Roman, sense. But the limitation that the Bible supposedly does not provide instructions for action has already been made as a precautionary measure in order to neutralize this point of view.

There are complaints that "conflicting interests of capital and labor" cause conflicts (page 26). However, it is not even a matter up for debate that the dualism between the factors underlying these conflicts is primarily to be understood from the point of view of the question of ownership and can therefore be overcome.

The closest weakness, which almost reflects naivety, is the repeated call for "state frameworks", "state action in economic affairs" (e.g., page 18), in the spirit of the social market economy. This applies in particular to the future of the social market economy in the Federal Republic of Germany, where "the further development of the social market economy is therefore essentially dependent on the ability and willingness of politicians to act, both nationally and, even more so, internationally" (page 71).

This statement completely overlooks the fact that conditions have changed dramatically in recent years. In the time of Ludwig Erhard, one could still justifiably speak of a national economy—a national economy in which the state could be assigned an important regulatory function. But what is to be done at the end of the millennium, when the economy is increasingly taking on continental and global dimensions, in which commercial enterprises increasingly elude national control? Do the authors of this memorandum not have an ear for the discussion among experts, where it says, for example, "The state's ability to act is diminishing.... Its capacity to act tends toward zero" (Bohret[69]) or "A state global control such as that striven for by Karl Schiller twenty years ago is no longer possible today. Multinational corporations and the competition between investment locations... lead... to the erosion of statehood"... (Scharpf[70]).

The question that needs to be answered is therefore primarily not that of the regulatory tasks of the state in a transnational economy but rather, who is supposed to exercise the necessary regulatory functions in an ultimately global economy when this role has largely slipped from the state and is slipping away—GATT, UN, Washington with a kind of PAX AMERICANA modelled on Rome? The paper makes none of this conscious.

Moreover, it is completely overlooked, at least not mentioned, that in the course of the internationalization of the economy, politics has for years been essentially limited to creating and maintaining a capital-friendly investment climate in the individual states and moreover to strengthening competitiveness. Both are efforts in which the concerns of people and nature are largely left by the wayside.

The climax of naivety or the pinnacle of insolence after all the negative stocktaking is reached with the statement:

"After forty years of development of the social market economy in the Federal Republic of Germany, it is

69 Frankfurter Rundschau 10th September 1991.
70 Ibid.

clear that this concept has proved its worth on the whole and has become a model of success" (page 32).

This statement is fatally reminiscent of the story of the rich grain farmer or landowner[71] who said to himself from his personal situation of meagre wealth, "Well done!... Eat and drink to your heart's content and enjoy life!"

When we speak of forty years, this means that this statement is to apply all the way into our recent past. If at least half of the time would be mentioned, but no, it must be forty years! This means that all the damage to man and nature and the apparent but fatal inevitabilities of our economic activities in the past and in the future are trivialities that have to be corrected by cosmetic correction. Here the whole critical preliminary work in the analysis section is not only called into question, its results are downplayed in an almost criminal way.

Seen as a whole, the memorandum is entirely in the spirit of Hananiah, one of the false prophets of Israel, and as such an opponent of Jeremiah. Of these it says in Jeremiah 23:14, "They strengthen also the hands of evildoers, that none doth return from his wickedness."

71 Luke 12.16 ff: "And he told them this parable: 'The ground of a certain rich man yielded an abundant harvest. He thought to himself, 'What shall I do? I have no place to store my crops.' Then he said, 'This is what I'll do. I will tear down my barns and build bigger ones, and there I will store my surplus grain. And I'll say to myself, 'You have plenty of grain laid up for many years. Take life easy; eat, drink and be merry.'''

Unfortunately there is nothing more to be said about this.

So the answers to our questions cannot be found with the Protestant Church in Germany.

Capital, Competition and Cooperation

In the search for a fairer economic system, the historical facts make it clear that the state-capitalist, planned-economy path not only nullifies any striving for freedom and self-determination,—basic needs of the mature human being—but is also too cumbersome, and quite simply works inefficiently.

However, this negative judgment of Eastern Europe's previous system does not automatically elevate the private capitalist system of the free market economy to the pinnacle of justice. While it is more liberal and flexible than the other, its negative sides are too obvious to be overlooked. International competition not only leads to an increasing pressure to perform. A growing number of so-called "under-performers", be they individuals, companies, entire regions or even countries, are unable to cope with this pressure. It also destroys nature and the environment without hesitation, often with all kinds of products that are all too short-lived or even completely superfluous. Just think of advertising and packaging, of agriculture in the European Community or of the megabit chip at IBM in Sindelfingen that had a production time of only three years. This was only half of the total life cycle of the product. It seems as if everything is produced that promises growth and profit. Everything that is useless and worthless to this short-sighted thinking and acting in categories of monetary value as the only measure is abandoned to ruin.

Certainly this madness cannot be explained mechanistically and overcome by coercive measures alone, because its roots reach very deep. Nevertheless, some very concrete steps towards more reason seem, according to historical development, to be due in our time.

Unfortunately, the great historical hour of the collapse of the Eastern European economic system was not used to realize future-oriented ideas of economic management. In a similar way as in Germany in 1848 in the political field, the reaction in this hour triumphed across the board. But this is less an act of stupidity or even malice. Rather, it is probably an almost inevitable consequence of the fact that in Christianity the task of the People of God as a pioneering society was hardly recognized by anyone, let alone taken seriously. Therefore, there is not only a lack of concrete ideas about a more just economy but even more a lack of concrete, convincing and comprehensible examples about which a comprehensive public discussion and an increase in awareness could have taken place. To a significant extent it is at best the anthroposophists who see the non-religious part of their task and destiny in seeking and taking new paths, including in business. And so the new things that would have had to be realized during the great upheaval remained largely unknown to the public and could not become an urgent public concern that could have been taken into account in the major political decisions.

Now we are at the point of locking the door after the horse has bolted. Obviously, the first thing to do is to point out once again and emphatically the destiny of the People of God as a pioneering society and then to try to sketch out the necessary new ways of shaping the economy:

Economic power is not inherited

We have learned in the past hundred years to consider the inheritance of political power in human history as obsolete. In Germany, the last political principalities disappeared in 1918. Today, if a descendant of a former chancellor, such as a biological grandson of Adenauer, were to claim to become chancellor by descent, everyone would laugh at him. Political power is no longer inherited today. This would no longer be appropriate to the general state of consciousness.

In contrast, the inheritance of economic power is still considered legitimate, even taken for granted by many. The descendants of the Flick dynasty exercise it just as naturally as the children of the successful but anonymous middle class, even if this is just as absurd as in the political sphere. Even if professional managers are employed almost everywhere today in active management positions, i.e., to a certain extent in the executive branch of the economy, the key positions in the supervisory bodies, i.e., in the legislative branch, are almost always filled in the traditional manner by the blood relatives of the previous generation of entrepreneurs or by their courtiers.

Sooner or later the development of public awareness will overcome this anachronism. However, more and more pioneers are needed who are willing to pave the way for this development and make corresponding power-political and financial "sacrifices".

No private ownership of joint ventures

In the not too distant past, it was conceivable and legitimate that individual persons, especially nobles, could call entire villages their own and dispose of them at will. Most documents proving the foundation and existence of villages and towns and thus forming the basis for the jubilees to be celebrated are purchase or gift deeds of nobles containing such municipal property. This is considered unimaginable nowadays. The communities of villages and towns today belong to nobody in the true sense of the word, as is the case with the common consciousness. It is true that taxes and duties are still payable. However, it is not, as in the past, primarily a private benefice for some privileged people that can be sold if necessary. In a healthy society, it serves merely to finance public tasks. Our consciousness has therefore developed its standards in this area as well. However, private property in company communities is still not publicly outlawed, even though its ostracism is clearly the developmental step in our consciousness that is due today. Our ideas concerning the ownership of municipal communities must therefore also be transferred to economic communities.

In Marxist-dominated thinking, ownership and rights of disposal over means of production are considered reprehensible. To simplify and generalize this way is probably a mistake. The ownership of and the right of disposal over things or material goods, regardless of their size or importance, seems to be perfectly acceptable. A decisive exception to this is land, especially because it is neither a human product nor reproducible. Therefore, there should be no ownership of land but only a temporary usufruct—i.e. rights of use, as in the case of the *commons*. This restriction does not apply to all other things and material goods, so that they can retain their commodity character.

As soon as people form an operating community using production resources, however, the picture changes. Since there should never be a right of disposal over people, because otherwise man is violated in his dignity and degraded to an object—to the thing—only a right of disposal of people over things can be legitimate. The decisive difference, then, lies in the question whether it is a matter of things or material goods, or more precisely, of objects that can be multiplied more or less at will. Then it is a commodity that can be traded and sold within the framework of free economy. But as soon as human beings become an essential part of the object of trade, its quality changes so dramatically that it can no longer be an object of trade. A machine or a workshop can be sold but a company or part of a company cannot. A business or part of a business can never be an object. Man, who works with the accumulation of machines or other equipment, is the subject and thus cancels the character of the equipment as an object. In concrete terms this means that an operating community can ultimately only make decisions affecting its existential fate together, ideally by consensus. However, this does not mean that it can ever become a commodity.

The logical consequence of this point of view is the statement, that in the present form there can not exist possession and ownership of enterprises where besides the "owner" other people are employed. Presumably, similar to land, there can be only temporary rights of use, usually for the duration of the employment but probably for life at most. It is obvious that the classic separation of the employer and the employee will become obsolete. The employee, at least the permanent employee of the core workforce, would become a co-entrepreneur. Only for marginal employees, such as temporary workers, the hitherto generally accepted term of employee would probably continue to apply.

Neutralization of working capital

The neutralization of working capital by creating foundations as capital carriers is not new. Yet it continues to lead a Cinderella-like existence in Western society. This could be brought to an end if foundations were systematically promoted through tax measures, especially in the case of inheritance. Since capital accumulation is a central social concern, it would be entirely conceivable to leave this path untaxed, provided that, as with foundations, it takes place entirely outside the realm of private income (and reserve) accumulation. The basic idea of a reduced tax rate for retained earnings, i.e., with no distribution of dividends, as is common today with corporate income tax for corporations, for example, would thus merely be developed further.

Since this goal is not discernible in any of the major parties in the Federal Republic (the SPD is completely paralyzed after the corporate bankruptcies of the trade unions on this issue), the responsibility today lies primarily with the owners of capital—current and future. This applies in particular to all those who, without having to forego an adequate livelihood and thus without real sacrifices, could renounce individual rights of power and disposal of at least parts of their million-dollar fortunes. This applies even if only by means of an appropriate will, i.e. in the event of death.

In earlier centuries, the rich left millions of dollars in assets to church institutions. What are they doing today? They hoard and hoard and never get enough, even after they are long dead.

They do not seem to understand that such a renunciation is not about the laborious fulfillment of high social-ethical standards with the character of divine laws. Rather, it is about liberation from one's own enslavement, a liberation that goes hand in hand with such an attempt to prepare a place for divine justice on earth.

It would be high time for Christians to begin to address this issue and say a clear word in favor of the creation of foundations.

For decades in India, Vinobe Bhave, a companion of Gandhi, has convinced many large landowners on his travels through the country to cede at least part of their land without coercion. In this way, hundreds of thousands of hectares of land could be transferred in a kind of "gentle" land reform. When will we begin to take on a similar task with the capital owners?

The Bible sufficiently supports our argumentation, since the question of ownership of land (the most important means of production in the predominant agriculture of the time) was an important topic not only in the Hebrew Bible but also for Jesus. Already in the Mosaic laws God says:

Mine is the land,
and you are strangers and sojourners before me.

This directive, this commandment, this law alone makes it clear that land ownership in the modern sense, that is, in the sense of a commodity that can be sold and bought, was inconceivable in ancient Judaism (as it was, incidentally, in many other peoples). Property was never more than a usufruct, a right of use, because land was not subject to the unrestricted human right of disposal. People could not imagine this any more than we can imagine the air as property today.

The story of Naboth[72], whose vineyard King Ahab wanted to buy, also relevant here. His answer:

The Lord forbid it me,
that I should give the inheritance
of my fathers unto thee.

is to be understood only against the background of the right of usufruct and not the property as a commodity. The same is true of Jesus' parable of the "wicked vine-growers,"[73] in which the tenants had

72 1. Kings 21.
73 Matt. 21.33 ff.

chased away or killed all the messengers of the owner, including his son, in order to gain usufruct because of neglect of the owner's duties. According to the understanding of law at the time, this neglect would have automatically resulted in the loss of the right to usufruct after a certain period of time and thus the transfer of usufruct to the tenants.

These three examples alone clearly show that the Israelite land law was quite different from the (pre-Christian) Roman one, which still shapes our thoughts and actions today. This is despite the fact that in almost all cultures, including the Germanic one, we had a similar understanding of land law as the ancient Israelites.

If we take the two points described above together, we can see that economic power should not be inheritable and that ownership of and rights of disposal over operating communities cannot be reconciled with a contemporary view of man. Boundary areas that require special regulation arise in small businesses and, in the founding generation, also in larger companies and the personal union of entrepreneurs and capital owners that is often encountered in such cases. As long as this personal union exists and is associated with unlimited private liability in the case of pure partnerships, as is customary in the case of sole proprietorships and general partnerships, the previous standards are still most justifiable. This is the case as long as speculative sales and purchases of joint ventures cannot occur in the end.

However, capital formation would be made more difficult in this way because it is also private income generation in these companies and must therefore be taxed accordingly. Only the separation of the entrepreneurial function from capital ownership and the restriction of risks to capital ownership without endangering the rest of the assets creates a completely new situation that requires new solutions in the manner described.

The cooperative plays a special role in the question of capital rights. In this legal form, friends and employees raise the necessary working capital or at least a sufficient base stock for it. If necessary, these funds are procured by a bank and guaranteed and paid off by the investor. The decisive evaluation criterion is the fact that such shares must never be traded as a commodity and therefore must never become an object of speculation. If a shareholder wants to withdraw for whatever reason, the shares are quasi repurchased by the cooperative (and only by it) and this usually at nominal value. Thus, the shares are never traded in public and are therefore not subject to speculation.

Even if not much is left of the spirit of those who originally fought for the legal form of the cooperative, the way itself is still forward-looking. A major handicap, however, is that it is not remotely possible to meet the capital requirements that are usually quite large today. The process of capital concentration almost inevitably goes hand in hand with our mismanagement of money and capital. In the time since the currency reform, only a small minority has accumulated the necessary funds to finance larger projects. If a job in Germany today requires on average an investment of at least a quarter of a million marks, this is far more than the average citizen is able to afford, or to borrow and repay for such a purpose.

Yet our insight leads even further. It is not only becoming unthinkable to inherit economic power. In fact, it should neither be granted nor claimed, because no one should have power over other people if human dignity is not to suffer on both sides.

The I-Thou relationship is lost in the process. Within power structures the ruler rises to the superhuman and reduces the other to the subhuman—the object. This creates an I-It relationship that blocks the process of becoming human on both sides[74].

The question of human scale

Unfortunately, most of the discussions about the issues raised here usually ignore the question of human scale. It remains the merit of E. F. Schumacher, who, especially with his book "Small is Beautiful1", has pointed out its enormous importance.

When trying to be considerate of human scale, there are basically two essential aspects—speed and size.

The importance of speed, i.e. the speed of all activities, but especially of change, is clearly shown by the development in the former GDR. There, regardless of the time needed to develop political awareness and the ability to think and act economically, a hasty connection was made that will most likely have catastrophic consequences. Even in business studies, where much less dramatic changes are involved, we no longer speak

74 See also under "Right of Command and Self-Determination.

of massive, revolutionary changes—from one day to the next, so to speak. Rather, we speak of organizational development, i.e. a continuous process of change, in which the time required for the development of a person's consciousness and the resulting change in behavior is taken into account. That is the one point.

The astrophysicist Peter Kafka[75] has investigated the mode of action of evolutionary processes and has examined the question why human development has had such catastrophic consequences, especially in the past fifty years, whereas evolution has led to far fewer major crises in the past. He describes one of the most important insights that Kafka came up with as "leisureliness". In evolution, the best path was calmly chosen from the myriad of possibilities for further development and then taken. Today, an almost insane hectic pace characterizes all steps of development. And it is above all demanded and shaped by our money multiplication mania and by pathological competition.

When it comes to the other point of necessary consideration of human scale, it is necessary to deal with the question of the optimal size of organizational structures.

It is a truism that man can only develop and exercise responsibility within a manageable framework. As soon as this framework is broken, irresponsibility and the sense of entitlement grows. Both go hand in hand with a kind of "market economy" thinking—the permanent attempt to achieve as much as possible for

75 Peter Kafka, Das Grundgesetz vom Aufstieg, München

oneself with as little effort as possible. This can be observed particularly clearly in the case of insurance and insurance-like services. It corresponds to our market-economy thinking to achieve the highest possible price for one's own performance and to pay as little as possible for the necessary external service. The history of the former GDR also provides deterrent examples of the excesses in this area.

The development of the ability and willingness to acquire and exercise responsibility thus depends crucially on whether the spaces within which responsible action is to be taken remain manageable in size. They remain manageable and correspond to the human measure, if the people, opposite whom responsibility is to be acted, are and remain humans and do not sink to numbers and figures. They remain human beings as long as they have a name, a face and a fate for the one who is to act responsibly with them. As long as the counterpart has a name, a face and a destiny, it is—as everyone knows—much more difficult to act inhumanely. It is therefore not seldom the case that the intention is clearly to go beyond this framework in terms of organization in order to be able to act inhumanely. This can be observed in planned "redundancy" or—more honestly expressed—dismissal actions as well as in war.

In order to be able to combine larger units even when taking these principles into account, it is sufficient—as can be observed in many cases today—to equip smaller, manageable units as "profit centers" with a high degree of autonomy. These can be under "self-government" and self-responsibility. They can be networked, whereby according to the principle of subsidiarity, power and responsibility are only shifted "upwards" to the extent that they can no longer be perceived and exercised "downwards", i.e. in the community itself. So we are not talking about unrealistic dreams but rather about organizational possibilities. In many cases, these are already reality today, at least in some areas.

At some point we have to understand that in our organizational structures man has to become the measure of all things and not money. Though this of course does not invalidate the law of nature, according to which every organism has to supply or generate at least as much energy (in our example money) in the long run as it consumes.

The principle according to which man is the measure of all things does not only apply to our organizational structures. It applies equally to the result of our work, such as the goods or services offered. The question has to be answered whether it serves man or harms him. This issue should not be addressed by a governmental supervisory authority (although often enough there is no other way out) but by the acquisition community itself.

However, this whole question must not be related to humans only in a narrow sense. Ultimately it refers to the whole creature and environment. After all, man is no more than a member of creation, who is affected by the well-being of the whole of nature as much as anything else.

Solidarity-based competition and social market economy

Every social economic doctrine oriented to human beings, from Christian ethics to the so-called Freiburg School and the social market economy, for which the name Ludwig Erhard stands in our country, has so far assumed that the free market economy is amoral in itself. The market laws of supply and demand, which determine the price, do not take into account the needs of people and nature. It is therefore common belief that the fulfillment of minimum social and ecological requirements should be ensured by means of coercive measures imposed by the state. The state-organized society is thus assigned one of the most important social tasks.

In recent years, however, we have observed that the national regulatory framework is being increasingly undermined by the business community. The transnational corporations have begun to locate their production facilities through global planning in such a way that they are hindered as little as possible by the respective national regulatory policy. This has led to a disparity in relocation to sites with the least possible social and ecological regulation. Initially, this differential was used primarily by the large transnational corporations. The advancing Europeanization and globalization of the economy prompted more and more companies, ultimately even the globally oriented SMEs, to follow the example of the transnational ones. This increasingly undermined the regulatory function of nation-state governments. The economy's search for "optimal" locations is less and less inhibited or even hampered.

However, this insight leads to highly problematic consequences not only for the company management itself. It is also increasingly providing national governments with a cheap excuse to postpone their regulatory tasks until the last possible moment. In the Federal Republic of Germany, for example, the 1938 revision of the Working Hours Act has been repeatedly abandoned. It would appear that the current government is completely abandoning it in the face of the imminent large Western European single market. Although the old Working Hours Act from 1938 was actually aimed at a war economy with the most unrestricted availability possible of so-called workers. In the late 1980s, the government's initial draft went even further, but in its present version it seemed hardly enforceable against the workers' side, even in the Christian Democratic Union (CDU). The draft still provided for an 8-hour day and a 6-day week as the rule. Now the discussion about this law has been quietly and shamefully ended. The reference to wage autonomy and the associated possibility of regulation is an all too cheap excuse for the state's omissions, especially when one knows that at least the half of all employers are exempt from the obligation to comply with collective agreements simply because they are not organized in appropriate associations.

The generally cherished hope that the European Community would be able to adopt a so-called Social

Charter with legal validity is deceptive. This Social Charter has indeed been formulated. However, it has only the character of a recommendation with which everyone can proceed at will.

The regulatory boundaries drawn by nation-state governments are decaying and are increasingly disappearing in a transnational economy. Thus, a long-cherished wish of the economy for deregulation (i.e., the dismantling of state restrictions) without legislative measures is being fulfilled simply through laissez-faire. However, when we read the statements of the business leaders, we cannot close our minds to the impression that they are like Goethe's sorcerer's apprentice who complained, "Those I called, the spirits, I cannot get rid of now." In any case, the so-called Stuttgart Declaration contained the following statement by the top managers of international corporations invited to a conference in 1990 by Lothar Späth, then Prime Minister of Baden-Württemberg:

"In an increasingly interdependent world, binding rules must be enacted and enforced by appropriate supranational institutions in the fields of antitrust law, competition law, intellectual property law and environmental standards"[76].

The fact that the social questions remain excluded thereby corresponds to the view of the employers. Overall, however, it is clear that these gentlemen are seriously concerned about the danger of relapsing into the style of early capitalism. It is highly doubtful, how-

76 Press release from the "Schwarzwälder Bote" of April 23, 1990.

ever, whether the supranational regulatory structures they are striving for can be created, regardless of whether they are to be located at the GATT or the UN.

The code of honor—the beginning of a further development

A reasonable way out of this dilemma seems to be to negotiate. Besides the national laws and collective agreements, it seems reasonable to negotiate codes of honor in individual areas that overlap them in a matrix-like manner and have similar binding force, in order to avoid at least the worst excesses of early capitalist economy.

However, since they do not have the force of law and cannot be enforced by court or police measures, the only way to ensure compliance with them is refusal (i.e., strike and refusal to accept) and the associated public ostracism.

For example, let us start with relatively simple problems, in the sense of a practice area. It would be conceivable that all tire manufacturers in the world would agree to refrain from producing tires on Sundays in order to avoid competitive disadvantages of individual locations. Initiators and negotiating partners for such codes of honor should not only be the companies themselves. They should be all those affected or their representatives, i.e. employers, employees, unions and probably also the churches. In order to avoid cartel-like agreements, for example at the expense of consumers, such negotiations should be conducted in public and their results published.

Evidently, there is an ever-weaker regulatory function of the state and the ever-increasing damage caused by unrestrained international competition. This makes it inevitable that cross-border agreements and arrangements on working conditions, types and quantities of production, etc. between producers and consumers will become necessary. Especially so if reason and the careful treatment of people and nature are not to be sacrificed completely to the detriment of all.

Anthroposophic social ethics sees the aim of this development as an associative economy, in which agreements within a sector are intended to prevent the excesses and inhumanities of today. Even if some questions and doubts remain unanswered, the basic insight is undisputed—only the path to more or less voluntary restrictions through insight and agreement is open if the cancerous growths of the international economy are to be contained.

In any case, in the development phase that is now due, the unrestricted free competition that is overwhelming everything today must be complemented and thus restricted by cooperation. It seems to be a matter of bringing the two goals together into one polarity, into a coexistence of seemingly irreconcilable opposites.

To repeat it again, in military strategy, we have long since learned to think in terms of security partnership categories. This means that our security is no greater than the security of the potential adversary. After all, if the potential adversary felt increasingly threatened, he could be prompted to react shortsightedly and take desperate steps to the detriment of all. Today, security partnership is a declared goal, at least in the East-West conflict. We have not yet developed anything comparable in economic thinking. This would mean that in all economic decisions, the vital interests of all those involved, including the respective opponents, must be taken into account, regardless of whether these are competitors, customers, employees or public welfare.

The example of economic systems makes it even clearer than elsewhere that we are contemporaries of a great upheaval. For thousands of years, mankind has been convinced that social problems can only be "solved" by a power elite forcing "solutions" through the use of power, domination and force. Roman imperialism stands symbolically in the Western world as the epitome of this way of thinking and acting. At the height of this imperialism, the Jewish Messiah Jesus arose from the traditions of his people as the antagonist of the Roman Caesar and taught and lived a "salutary alternative" to this way of thinking and acting[77]. His seed is now, almost two thousand years later, finally beginning to sprout in the non-religious realm as well. The power-thinking is at an end. On its way the problems can finally no longer be solved. It is true that the power elites in the economy (and politics) still cling to the old methods and seek salvation on the one hand in ever larger power structures and thus succumb to gigantomania. On the other hand they call for "supra-

77 See also, Haller, Die heilsame Alternative, Wuppertal 1989.

national (power) structures" (see above). And yet it is clearly evident that these paths also lead astray.

The ethical side of our economic activity must therefore continue to develop from the (originally state-guaranteed and secured) social market economy. This economy is increasingly losing or has already lost the adjective "social" and is moving towards a self-regulating "solidarity-based" market economy that ensures the observance of ethical norms even without state intervention. On wonders where this will all come from, it may take a long time for this process to achieve appropriate goals. Unfortunately, there is no reason for optimism. This does not change the fact, however, that we have to start with this task. After all, as is well known, even the longest journey begins with the first step.

This first step means that, starting in the small "alternative" area, new economic structures are created in an attempt to do justice to the insights described above. This is the so-called "third way". Even if it seems to be no longer viable for some masterminds of further development after the collapse of the economic structures in the East, it is probably the only way—however laborious and protracted—to develop and realize alternatives to our murderous economic system.

Real Estate Ownership and Right of Abode

Just like the situation in the former GDR before and after zero hour, developments on the housing market make it clear that the question of house or apartment ownership has not yet found a satisfactory answer, at least not to an extent that would have been politically significant.

The fact that land is considered a commodity in the capitalist world is a major error with dramatic, existentially threatening consequences for those affected. In the free market economy, as is well known, the price is determined by supply and demand. If now the financial assets grow massively by the interest and compound interest effect, then they look inevitably again and again for safe investment and new increase. For conservative private and institutional investors real estate possession is considered thereby to be a safe haven. The demand of these financial assets to grow continuously during economically more or less stable times is however confronted with a supply that cannot become larger to the same extent. Although it is possible to build more or less large residential units on existing plots of land, one (as every builder-owner knows) essential cost factor, namely the land required for this, is a factor that cannot be increased. In any case, the area of land available for construction cannot be enlarged to any significant extent. It is predetermined and largely unchangeable. The consequence of this is that on the land market, as the basis of the housing market, a more or less unchanging supply is confronted with a tendency of growing demand. The inevitable consequence of this is that land prices are growing almost continuously. Gross wages and salaries in the Federal Republic of Germany have increased more than sixfold on average since 1960. However, the prices of building land have risen by a factor of 15 on average over the same period.[78]

Even in countries such as Switzerland, with its broad prosperity also for most of the working population, this development means that well-paid skilled workers have to give up apartments in which they have lived with their families for many years because they can no longer pay the rent. The development of rents, which is almost inevitably linked to real estate prices, is running away from the income trend almost everywhere and hits the lower income groups with great severity. As everyone knows, this applies not only to most parts of Switzerland but also in the same way to Germany. The old rule of thumb, according to which an apartment may cost a quarter to a third of income, has often become a pipe dream. In many cases, the entire second income in a family serves more or less exclusively to finance living—if it is sufficient at all.

78 Figures by Helmut Creutz according to documents of the Bundesbank and the Federal Statistical Office in Germany.

The fact is that the price explosion on the real estate market benefits above all those who own living space as a financial investment and as an object of speculation but not or not only for their own use. This is demonstrated by a simple example. If a certain dwelling grows in purchase price from 200.000 to 500.000 Marks, then that does not benefit those who use this dwelling as only their own real estate possession. If they would sell the dwelling and skim off the price increase, then they would hardly have money left, because they would have to buy a dwelling of course again. This dwelling would most likely have a similar price development and would therefore eat up the gain. The increase falls only to those who have real estate possession beyond the dwelling used by themselves.

The problem is basically neither new nor unknown. In the postwar period, all political groups have demanded and sought a reform of land law. This also applies to the people of the CDU and CSU, as can be read in their first basic programs. Why the cloak of silence has been shamefully covering up this question for years now remains incomprehensible. Even for the simplest mind, not only the rent burden but also examples like that of the old Finck in Munich are clear enough. As is well known, this banker, who has since passed away, has become a billionaire without the slightest economic achievement. In wise foresight of Munich's structural development, he simply bought up land, kept it for a long time and then sold it again as expensive building land. So land speculation has made him a very rich man. In the economic sense this is pure parasitism, because he himself did not generate the slightest economic value.

However, this undesirable development has now progressed so far that fundamental changes are due. Politicians are making every effort to avoid breaking their taboos on the land issue. They are therefore forced to keep at least the most serious misguided developments under control by means of all kinds of patchwork. This begins with tax incentives for building society savings and housing construction in general and ends with the payment of housing benefit in the sense of social assistance. In the long run, however, this patchwork will not solve the problem. Nevertheless, it will probably still take some time before politicians dare to tackle the fundamental issues. The task will thus first of all hang more on those who understand their Christian or humanity as belonging to a pioneer society and derive from it the task to go new ways. This also applies to the housing market, as far as they are able to do so due to the circumstances, for example home ownership or other assets.

In the sense of ancient non-Roman land rights, there are two things involved. On the one hand the ownership of real estate should be neutralized. Land is not a commodity whose price is determined according to the laws of the market economy and is therefore subject to speculation. Rather, land and soil, like air, should only be distributed and managed in an appropriate manner. In the same way, the ownership of houses and apartments should be redefined on the basis of a new land law. Thus, it is neither private nor state property. We have had sufficiently bad experiences in both the East and West. It can only be a question of rights of use, i.e. rights of development and housing. These should essentially differ from traditional property rights in two areas: On the one hand, a time limit, for example for life, instead of the claim to eternity that is customary today. On the other hand, the exclusion of speculation, which is promoted above all by the fact that home ownership over and above personal use is conceivable, possible and customary as a "capital investment".

Ludwig Gruber tells the story of highland Indians in Bolivia1, where at the wedding the young couple is provided with a building plot by the community, on which the wedding party then builds a small residential house from beams and mud bricks. The life span of this house is about as long as the life of the spouses, so it is usually demolished after their death. This picture illustrates the ideal situation.

Ideally, nobody should be the owner of land. The municipality should only act as administrator and mediator. Since it will be a long way to this goal, ownership and the associated rights of disposal would have to be transferred to small, decentralized societies—associations, cooperatives or foundations. The same companies could also become "owners" of the houses and apartments and grant rights of use. However, this would require that the right to sell property rights be excluded by statute or by some other legal basis.

Roughly speaking, there are three ways to use the apartments. The first is the classical rent, in which the costs of maintenance and renovation are essentially borne by the landlord and financed from the income.

Secondly a rent with the obligation for maintenance and renewal on the part of the tenant. This second way would thereby rather become a right of residence with monthly "remuneration". Thirdly, the actual right of residence, which in many respects corresponds to the English "lease". This right of abode would take the place of classical ownership. The differences lie mainly in the time limit of the rights of use. These rights of use would be for life or for the length of the biblical jubilee and sabbath year cycle—six or 49 years, with an option for an extension if necessary.

The renunciation of inheritance would thus represent a significant difference to the right of ownership. This need not necessarily be a decisive disadvantage. On the one hand, the apartment is sold often enough during generational change and inheritance, because it does not seem to be usable for the next generation for whatever reason. In such cases the problem simply becomes a question of money. On the other hand, it should be possible to keep the costs for rent and housing rights so favorable by waiving interest (in whole or in part) that, taking into account the more or less developed consciousness of the buyers, the financial disadvantages for the children at the time of inheritance are kept within reasonable limits by additional financial safeguards, such as life insurance in favor of the descendants. However, it must not be overlooked that the insurance companies have been among the worst sinners of our misguided money and capital economy up to now, especially in the so-called real estate market.

It seems to be of decisive importance that land loses its commodity character and is withdrawn from speculation, as is the case today with shares in cooperatives.

Also the hereditary lease, which can still be found here and there, at least partially follows this path. In any case, the building ground is not treated as a commodity. Rather, the structural use of a plot of land is permitted in return for the regular, approximately annual payment of a ground rent for a limited period of time, approximately 75 years. The amount of this ground rent corresponds to a low interest rate on the commercial value of the land at the time of the conclusion of the contract. This is the weakness of the concept, as the market value is or can be influenced by land speculation.

According to a ruling by the Federal Court of Justice, the ground rent may not exceed an average value of the increase in the cost of living and gross wages[79]. It is therefore not subject to speculation like the starting price, i.e. the market value, but remains parallel to the costs and income and thus within reasonable limits.

Here too, not only is a feasible path being mapped out but it is also already being taken on a small scale. It is only necessary to reconsider it and to realize it on a growing scale.

79 Information from the Sozialwissenschaftlichen Gesellschaft in Northeim 142.

Law and Freedom

After all that has gone before, the impression must inevitably arise that the responsible person is burdened with a whole lot of "you should" or "you should not". In the end, therefore, the task remains to counter this misunderstanding and to deal with the question of how to shape reality, law, order and personal freedom.

One of the most common prejudices about Judaism is the view that its character is primarily determined by the demand for submission to strict biblical laws. This opinion is fostered in Christianity by the predominance of Pauline thought. As is well known, Paul had advocated liberation from the law through faith in Christ [80]. He was therefore involved in considerable controversy with the Jewish Christian community in Jerusalem. In fact, for a superficial Christianity, this Pauline line often becomes the starting point for a conviction that Jesus' disagreements with the country's leaders stem from diametrical contrasts, in which Jesus stands for freedom from the law and the others for submission to the law. This conviction is not tenable from the traditions. For all the generosity that Jesus showed in observing the law, his statement that even

80 Especially in the letter to the Romans.

the last iota of the law must be fulfilled[81] remained clear.

The actual historical development makes the error about Judaism very clear. While Christianity quickly dogmatized certain principles of faith, the attempted enforcement or combating of which often led to religious wars and murder and manslaughter, Judaism soon came to realize that there were as many interpretations of the Torah as there were Jews. In the famous disputes between scholarly Jews and Christians in the Middle Ages, this became clear time and again. Even then, the Jewish side showed much more mental agility and individual freedom in all these questions than the opposite side.

This seems to me to be an essential error, not only by Franz Alt, but also by Hanna Wolff, who is able to recognize this openness and individuality only in Jesus but not in Judaism in general. In reality, the differences described by these authors are, on the one hand, general, recurrent inner-Jewish rabbinical conflicts about the interpretation of the laws—e.g., which actions are permissible on the Sabbath—and, on the other hand, the age-old conflict inherent in all religious communities between law and freedom, between dogma and change born of the spirit and the immediate, overwhelming experience of God.

This conflict is found not only within Judaism but equally within Christianity. It is also found in other religions and religion-like ideologies. In communism, for example, the writings and speeches of Marx and Lenin

81 Matt. 5.17.

were and are highly stylized and dogmatized into quasi-divine revelations.

People, and especially the power elites, always tend to enshrine the traditions and statements of extraordinary personalities in generally binding dogmas with the force of law, compelling them to be observed. The willingness to submit to charismatic leaders and the rules they establish seem to encourage the temptation of such personalities to assume divine power and the corresponding rights of instruction. And if these themselves do not succumb to the temptation, as was quite obviously the case, for example, with Jesus, then for the sake of their own benefit and convenience alone, conflict-shy, anti-dialogue and power-hungry followers make sure that the dogmatization and the exclusive administration of salvation by them, which is usually connected with it, is not called into question by the others. This is classical conservatism, which can be found among the Orthodox Jews as well as in the Vatican, among the Evangelicals, the Pietists, and the Communists.

This conservatism is of course not fundamentally reprehensible. After all, every community, from the religious community to state society, needs an internal order that also regulates the way people live together. It is therefore not surprising that after his abolition of the Jewish system of order, Paul recommended his followers to submit to the state order of Roman law[82]. Order must be but it must not be allowed to freeze to

82 This is also made clear above all in the Epistle to the Romans.

the extent that religious and interpersonal experiences from long gone times and their interpretation by some privileged person become dogmas and laws in the long run. Rather, it is a matter of including the traditions in a dialogue of the living and thus making them the basis and source of the further development of order—the eternal search for justice and truth. In this way, space is created for the correction and improvement of misjudgments and errors of both previous generations and one's own. This acknowledges that the absolute and objective truth is at best only fragmentarily accessible to man but that his subjective truths on the path to liberation are in constant need of joint reflection, correction and improvement. This without losing sight of and respect for the great traditions, which are, after all, saturated with the inspirations, dreams, hopes, longings, experiences, joy and suffering of many generations. In this way, they receive content and meaning that often reach the quality of the sacred and whose concerns we cannot escape. However, this does not turn them into an absolute authority that must not be questioned. Rather, they appear as a mysterious treasure, the deeper contents of which are difficult to access and are only hesitantly revealed without compulsion.

It cannot be overlooked that the living individual interpretation of law and order in Roman power thinking—with its claim to eternity in its attempted fixation—is given much less space in the long run than the Jewish or even the Germanic sensibilities. In order to recognize this, it is sufficient to compare the Roman imperialist legal systems from CORPUS IURIS

CIVILIS to the Napoleonic Code up to the present day, with their attempted absolutisation of the Basic Law in Germany, for example. This is in contrast to the jurisprudence of the rabbis based on the various interpretations of the Torah or the Anglican way of thinking, which finds its particular expression in common law.

The restriction of all human testimonies to the fragmentary and subjective, of course, also applies to this book. This does not preclude me from defending my opinion with all my strength and passion. Quite the contrary. But I am insightful enough to understand that my perceptions are very subjective, at least in places, and will continue to require dialogue in the future in order to provide useful building blocks for the way forward.

Even if many of the experiences to be included in this process are timeless, it must be recognized that this is mostly true only for the content but not for the form. This means that even if we concede timeless divine dimensions to the content of such an experience, it must be questioned again and again, which form this content has to find in order to become experienceable and comprehensible in the here and now. The form may have to be changed, even if the content remains the same.

The problem and the most widespread misunderstanding are most clearly visible in the so-called Ten Commandments. In the traditions, a prefix in which God identifies himself as liberator and redeemer[83] is

83 "I AM your God, who brought you out of the land of

followed by a whole series of "Thou shalt..." and "Thou shalt not..." in the German language Bible. They are generally understood as conditions of the law. In fact, the whole story means that when man sets out on the path of liberation from his dependencies by God, he becomes free from all that is harmful and no longer does it, because he no longer has to do it compulsively. As Ernst Lange had already understood, who referred to the Ten Commandments as the Ten Freedoms, it is more a question of Ten Liberations than of the legal compulsion of Ten Commandments. That is why Martin Buber does not speak of the law but of the instruction of God. And this applies equally to the Jew and the Christian (and to everyone else). The emphasis is thus always on the search for God, as the parable of Jesus of the treasure in the field and of the especially beautiful pearl makes clear[84], and not on the compulsions of the law. Even if, of course, the one conditioned the other, just as in this parable the renunciation of everything superfluous is needed to achieve the great goal.

For example, if the so-called Ten Commandments are actually about ten liberations, then they stem from man's relationship with God. This is probably what Paul actually meant, even if this was and is misunderstood again and again. In the relationships of human beings with one another, on the other hand, which include the entire social life, corresponding command-

Egypt, out of the house of bondage" (according to Martin Buber).

84 Matt. 13.44 ff.

ments, prohibitions—that is, laws—are naturally indispensable for peaceful coexistence. (However, they do not have to be (pre-Christian) Roman ones). For the individual human being, depending on his relationship or love for God, for himself and for other people, these then become freedoms or constraints. They are therefore either freedom from burdens or actual burdens.

How to find and walk the path to liberation from dependencies is a completely different question. The Jewish proverb "In memory lies the secret of salvation" shows where the answer to this question can be found. The search requires an examination of collective history and its teachings and traditions as well as its individual component, the part that has shaped us personally. This also includes the willingness to engage with one's own feelings, especially those that are suppressed.

Here, too, it is a matter of an internal and an external, of a departure that aims at a change, a conversion both internally and externally, just as every therapy for the desired inner change almost always requires a change in behavior and life circumstances.

All the things described and enumerated here should not be understood as an attempt to work out and impose new legal constraints. Rather, it is an attempt to sketch due and feasible steps of external liberation as a consequence and as a prerequisite for the experience of internal liberation.

In fact, it is a question of both consequence and precondition. In a kind of cybernetic control loop, they mutually condition and follow each other. This becomes evident not only in the story of the Exodus, where the experience of God from Sinai, the experience of meaning and the possible fulfillment of one's own inner destiny would be unthinkable without the step of the Exodus and the train through the desert. The same applies to the Christmas story of the shepherds and the so-called wise men of the Orient. Both groups had to leave the familiar for the encounter with the child and follow their dream against all reason. Here, too, the liberating experience of God comes only after the departure from the everyday and the traditional. It is actually self-evident that the divine impulse triggers the departure. Where else could it come from? Above all, the whole thing makes clear how the path runs. Impulse, insight, experience, encounter trigger the awakening and lead to new insight and experience and thus are able to trigger the new awakening. Always in the beginning is the encounter with the liberating and redeeming God. It is followed by the time of desert and darkness—and the responsible action—the action as a response to the liberating experience.

All too long and all too often in Christianity, the Sinai experience has been and still is pretended to take place directly at or even in the flesh pots of Egypt, that is, in prosperity and enslavement as the all too often price paid for prosperity. The talk of "cheap" grace has done much harm. It is simply a lie. Sinai and Egypt are mutually exclusive, even if, of course, in the sense described, the Sinai experience is not possible without the Egyptian experience, but presupposes it.

Anyone who becomes aware that he is—figuratively speaking—living in the slavery of Egypt, and who suffers from it, will have to go on—once, several times, again and again. Sinai lies outside, in front of us, beyond the desert, but it is worth the effort, because the way, as the story tells, is accompanied by God. Even if it is not always a God of close but also a God of distance.

It is not about the path of asceticism, which clouds faces with bitterness and grumpiness. It is about a path of liberation that can lead man from a four-legged reptile of inner and outer dependencies to the "glorious freedom of the children of God"[85] and make him an upright human being[86].

Is this law, is this instruction, is this insight? Everyone may call it what he wants. It is the way which man should take for his own sake, for the sake of his humanity, for the sake of his destiny.

Should he walk it also for the sake of the indwelling God?

85 Paul according to Romans 8, 21.

86 See also Leviticus 26.13:

"I am the LORD your God,
which brought you forth out of the land of Egypt,
that ye should not be their bondmen;
and I have broken the bands of your yoke,
and made you go upright."

The Emerging Deity

In Exodus, the second book of Moses, it is reported how the people of Israel built and worshipped the golden calf during the absence of Moses on Sinai and how the punishment announced by God was subsequently averted by the objection of Moses. It says there at the end, "Then the Lord refrained from carrying out his threat and did not destroy his people."

We can dismiss this story, as well as others of similar significance, as a document of a primitive conception of God. In addition to God acting in mysterious, often quite incomprehensible ways, we see a very human God, to whom emotional outbursts, even with terrible consequences, are not alien. This view cannot be dismissed. But it is not enough to dissolve the mystery of God described here, whose actions can be influenced by man. Presumably, the idea of God in the Hebrew Bible contains more than just a hint of the truth of God when it describes him as a nascent being with such stories for our human-earthly perception. Bonhoeffer says[87]:

"People go to God in His need, find him poor, reviled, without shelter and bread, see Him devoured by sin, weakness and death. Christians stand with God in His suffering. God goes to all people in their need."

87 Bonhoeffer, Widerstand und Ergebung, Munich, 1951

But God seems to be not only the mysteriously working and, beyond that, the suffering one that Bonhoeffer describes here. His participation in the fate of his creatures probably goes even further.

It actually appears as if God had not only progressively incarnated himself in the process of creation but on this path also progressively limited himself in his omnipotence to such an extent that it finally depends on man which characteristics of God become reality on earth.

The path of creation is quite obviously a path of growing freedom for creatures. It begins with the mineral with its an almost complete mechanical solidification, reaching to the plant with its ability to move, even if it remains essentially bound to its location. In the animal, the location-bound state is largely overcome but behavior and actions remain restricted by instinct and controlled by drives. Only humans are able to step out of the dullness of the unconscious instinct life into the freedom of consciousness and conscious action.

Of course, this freedom only reaches as far as God releases man from his omnipotence and control. The idea of an omnipotent God cannot be reconciled with the image of human freedom. And since, as the Bible makes clear again and again, God is a liberating God, and human freedom is the central concern, this means that God's working power is above all a serving and not a ruling power. It is therefore no more than an offer that leaves open the acceptance or rejection and also the way in which it is to be used—be it only in a more or less wide range of human freedom. It may well be that the divine goals on this earth will inevitably be realized. But the how and when seems to be largely open, because these goals manifest themselves as urges and as longing and not—mechanically-technically speaking—as a forceful connection that leaves no room for maneuver and thus no freedom of choice.

Accordingly, man is an autonomous, sovereign, mature being whose task it is to go his way in good and evil alone and with the help of his fellow men. He acts on his own responsibility. God gives him the strength for this. He fulfills his destiny, however, only when God's longing becomes his own.

Yet with it the greatness, dignity and importance of man is not yet fully grasped. According to the concept of God in the Hebrew Bible, man's task and responsibility go even further.

If, as our history shows, it requires the objection of man to prevent God from "making his threat come true," then man has not only unrestricted responsibility for his own behavior and deeds, thus also for Auschwitz. Beyond this, he is responsible for the transformation of the indwelling God, namely, for the fact that the manifestation of God on this earth, as far as a man is able to describe it in the space-time restriction imposed on him, develops from the primitive murderous revenge to the behavior. As Jesus described it in the so-called Sermon on the Mount, for instance. Accordingly, with the help of the divine powers offered to him, man has to walk a path of redemption for himself, for humanity, for the whole of creation—and for the indwelling God himself. He is thus an independent tool for the liberation of the indwelling God from the self-imposed prison of a low level of development.

As also the temptation story of Jesus shows, the dark, the "primitive" indwelling God needs and wants the inner resistance, the inner confrontation. This "primitive" God is indeed described in Jesus as the devil. However, in the Hebrew Bible, the devil is not a counter-God of equal rank as in everyday Christianity but one of the sons of God, as this becomes particularly clear in Job. Accordingly, the devil is a certain part, a certain side of the One God. In fact, it is only the common dualism that makes him a Christian devil. That is, when he is split off, and when we try to suppress his existence. In reality he corresponds to the dark side of God and awaits redemption on the path of liberation through man. Jesus teaches to transform evil by good. This happens when dualism becomes polarity through man as the connecting link.

C. G. Jung calls that which of it becomes visible in the human psyche the shadow and speaks of the necessity of its integration in the sense of this salvation. By this he means (only) the aspect that concerns the salvation of the person in question. However, seen as a whole it is the same process.

So we do not only experience the bright side of God, which we encounter above all in silence, an experience that John of the Cross, one of the great mystics, describes with "a gentle, silent glow. We also experience the dark side of the indwelling God but mostly in a painful way, pointing to a task to be solved. In this way we encounter God transcendently with his timeless love and also immanently as the becoming and transforming one. The one side can be described as masculine, the other as feminine and can probably be experienced, as Friedrich Weinreb, for example, means when he says that the feminine, the maternal side of God, the Shechina, accompanies man into earthly reality.

It seems, therefore, as if God's indwelling in his earthly creatures is connected with a limitation to their behavior and capacity to act. It seems as if the evolutionary process is also for the indwelling God an ascent from a twilight in the stone over the consciousness in man up to the height of his cosmic being with his all-encompassing love. In this evolutionary process the contribution of man seems to be indispensable. This is probably what the ancient Jews meant when they spoke of man's task to contribute to the unification of God with his Shechina, namely his indwelling reality[88]. Martin Buber writes about it: "My face is that of the creature."

The indwelling God, who is probably identical not only with the Jewish Shechina but also with the Great Mother, the Goddess of Nature, corresponds in his "consciousness" to the "consciousness" of the various members of creation and unfolds according to the higher development of man that he accompanies to a certain extent and thus corresponds to their respective state. Through the inherent longing for union, for unity, a fruitful tension is created as the driving force for further development, the path of salvation, the history of redemption.

88 cf. Martin Buber, Zwischen Zeit und Ewigkeit.

We know from in-depth psychology that Yahweh often reveals himself in dreams as an animal man, and Count Dürckheim reports from his therapeutic work how the split-off and repressed Great Mother eats her children. Here early forms of development become visible, which make its stages clear.

The organic evolution, which is essentially long since completed, is followed by the spiritual evolution, whose carrier and crystallization point is man. Symbolically speaking, he has his head in heaven and his feet on earth. He is the connecting link for the energy flow of the divine power between the cosmic and the earthly indwelling God and is responsible for overcoming dualisms and restoring the unity between the eternal, timeless and earthly time-bound. This unity manifests itself as an earthly-human polarity, i.e. above and below, light and dark, good and evil. And thus love "from above" meets the longing "from below. Its source is ultimately the same, even if the "from below" has taken on manifold and different forms on its way in creation, and manifests itself not seldom for man as "evil.

Thus man can experience both freedom and security, two of his basic needs. These can be compared with individuation and socialization, in the two aspects of God. The male principle of liberation on the one hand and the female principle of security on the other hand. This can be experienced in a positive way only through man's contribution to their unification.

The restriction of God's omnipotence in the sphere of man's earthly reality thus goes not only so far that God withdraws for the sake of man's freedom, so as not to seriously limit it. It even implies that the manifestation of God's unconditional love on this earth. Its experienceable reality is made dependent on man's behavior and actions in a way that, as our history shows, makes man in his special personalities, such as Moses in our history, appear more responsible, kinder and more merciful than God himself. Obviously, however, this is not simply a phenomenon. The earthly manifestation of just these divine traits of character seems indeed to depend on the fact that man "prepares a place for them" by his thinking, speaking, behavior and action. Otherwise it remains just a possibility but does not become reality. This is probably meant when there is mention of preparing the way for the Lord[89].

On this path, three stages are emerging which correspond to the three concepts of spirit, soul and body. The divine impulse, human possibilities and earthly reality. The divine impulse, the vision of the great harmony, in our image emanates from the transcendent God. It is the foundation of the divine history of salvation and the driving force of man. However, it is only one possibility, a possibility that will eventually become reality due to its inherent dynamics. Yet the how and when seems to be very strongly influenced by man. Mankind turns this possibility into concrete earthly reality. Thereby the request of the Our Father, "Thy will be done on earth as it is in heaven", becomes reality on earth. In doing so, man fulfills his destiny and thus unites the " higher" and the "lower" God.

89 e.g. Jes. 40.3.

Nevertheless, on this path of incarnation, aberrations are also possible. They consist above all in reifying the creative spirit and directing it outwards. It then no longer primarily serves the transformation of man and thus of his behavior but rather technical innovation and other materially founded ways of salvation. These mostly take on addiction-like forms and then correspond to the biblical idols.

Every human being is a microcosmic part of the cosmic drama. His personal abilities and difficulties reflect segments of the great evolution that each individual has as his or her very own task. Through his maturation process he contributes not only to his personal salvation but also to the salvation of the world and the salvation of the indwelling God. This is genuine worship—in the true sense of the word.

Thus man's freedom is accompanied by an almost divine dignity and an extraordinarily great responsibility. This makes him truly the guardian and steward of the earth, both in the small and the large. And it reaches up to his decisive influence on the realization of the divine vision and order with us.

Perhaps in this way the meaning and significance of the life of Jesus, as the first new man, as Franz Alt calls him, for earthly reality becomes clear in a special way. With him, the ambivalence of the perceivable God becomes clear in the fact that Jesus says that no one is good but God. And yet in the Lord's Prayer he asks not to be tempted by God. The special significance of this request is made clear by the fact that he does not express it in passing, so to speak in a subordinate clause, but that, according to tradition, he makes it a daily request in great prayer and thus a central concern. Thus he not only trusts God to do this but also believes that God is to be prevented from doing so by man's request. In this way, the divine dichotomy that exists for human perception can be eliminated.

Jesus also makes two things especially clear. On the one hand, the overwhelming importance of love, and on the other, how man has to face the greatest temptation that can arise from the insights described. Their special theme for Jesus, namely the question of power and violence, is not only at the beginning of his work —namely in the story of temptation—but also becomes the main theme at the last supper and thus gains legacy-like significance.

For man runs the risk of succumbing to the delusion of omnipotence. This could be observed especially with the German Nazis, who based their world view on a probably misunderstood Nietzsche, who, as is well known, spoke of the Übermensch (Superhuman). In the Jesuanic way of thinking, however, the "Übermensch" is the human being, who, although aware of his importance but also of his diminutiveness in the cosmic drama, consistently renounces power and, in all humility, tries to make the will of the transcendent God his own out of experienced love. In this way, he tries to contribute to the (re-) establishment of unity.

The special contribution of Jesus to his own salvation, to the salvation of the world and to the salvation of the indwelling God consisted in extracting from the various traditions and prophetic visions of the Hebrew Bible the strand of love, the image of God as a human being and, consequently, of non-violence and the renunciation of power as the actual divine goals. In the argument with the indwelling God (according to the Greek Bible with the devil or the tempter), he struggled for this strand not only to become the earthly guideline but also to become "incarnated" in it and thus became earthly reality for all salvation.

Christendom has only begun to understand this, as the disputes over questions of armament and governmental power and the dualism practiced in this context repeatedly make clear. And yet, through his life and teachings, Jesus has made a decisive contribution to overcoming this dualism and transforming it into a polarity, that is to say, into an arc of tension that includes both sides and thus makes them fruitful.

The dualism that Jesus overcame, but which is still dominant in most Christians, sees on the one hand a heavenly God of grace, mercy and love and the validity of the Sermon on the Mount derived from it for the inner and private life. On the other hand, it sees an earthly God "who let iron grow"[90] and of whom it was said on the military buckles, "God with us", that is, a

90 This refers to *The Vaterlandslied* (Song of the Fatherland), a patriotic poem written by Ernst Moritz Arndt in 1812. Verse one:

> "The god who made iron grow
> Did not want slaves;
> Therefore he gave sabre, sword and spear
> To man in his right hand;
> Therefore he gave him bold courage,
> The rage of free speech,
> So that he would prevail to the last drop of blood,
> Even unto death, in the struggle."

God who also blesses murder and manslaughter. Unfortunately, many of us are still subject to this dualism, even though the message of redemption from it is constantly on our lips.

Jesus, at the risk of his life, tried to overcome this dualism, this division and to restore unity in polarity. To do so, he had to "switch through" the unconditional love of God, dramatically experienced in the Jordan baptism, to unite the light and dark sides of himself—and God. It is not without reason that the stories of the baptism in the Jordan River and of the temptation in the desert in the traditions are the prelude to the public ministry of Jesus. They reflect the two aspects of God that are to be united such that the dark, the primitive, the indwelling "part" of God, bound to the evolutionary course of time, is brought closer to the timeless and eternal "part" of God. In terms of the earth-human perception, this corresponds to the transformation from dualism to polarity.

Does such a change of the common conception of God have a concrete influence on our state within the world and on our handling of reality or does it not represent more than a theological speculation detached from reality?

C. G. Jung tells the story of his encounter with the North American Pueblo Indians[91], which could be significant for this:

One of the Pueblo chiefs answered his question, "Do you think that what you do in your religion bene-

91 A. Jaffe, Erinnerungen, Träume, Gedanken von C. G. Jung, Olten, 1971.

fits the whole world? He answered, "After all, we are a people who live on the roof of the world, we are the sons of the Father Sun, and with our religion we help our Father daily to walk across the sky. We do this not only for ourselves, but for the whole world. If we can no longer practice our religion, the sun will not rise until ten years from now. Then it will be night forever."

Subsequently, C. G. Jung does, admittedly, first address European rationalism, out of which we "smile at Indian naivety and find ourselves sublime in our wisdom". But he continues and says:

"However, the fact that man feels able to respond fully to the overpowering influence of God and to give an essential return even to God is a proud feeling that elevates the human individual to the dignity of a metaphysical force. "God and us", this equivalent relationship probably underlies that enviable serenity. Such a man is in his place in the fullest sense of the word."

An alcoholic, for example, would have to experience a similar situation when he learns that his confrontation with his addiction resembles the temptation of Jesus in the desert. The tempter, however, on the one hand represents the dark side of God and not a split-off and downright challenging devil as counter-God. On the other hand—and this seems to be even more important—this dark God needs redemption as much as the alcoholic himself. His difficult path thus serves not only himself—which many have become completely indifferent to in this situation anyway—but also the salvation of the dark indwelling God. What he does or does not do, therefore, reaches beyond his own condition. Here, too, man is able to grow "to the dignity of a metaphysical force"— to repeat the words of C. G. Jung—in order to give his life a new meaning.

In concrete terms, this would mean that while man should love his addiction and the God of his addiction, his therapy and worship should aim to stop falling into that dependency. Here, too, the parallel to Jesus' story of temptation makes it clear what is at stake.

www.ingramcontent.com/pod-product-compliance
Lightning Source LLC
LaVergne TN
LVHW091413190726
843491LV00006B/1414

* 9 7 8 3 9 4 9 1 9 7 1 6 1 *